TAPESTRY

GET IT?
GOT IT!

Listening to Others/
Speaking for Ourselves

TAPESTRY

The **Tapestry** program of language
materials is based on the concepts
presented in *The Tapestry Of
Language Learning: The Individual
in the Communicative Classroom* by
Robin C. Scarcella &
Rebecca L. Oxford.

Each title in this program focuses on:

Individual learner strategies and
instruction

The relatedness of skills

Ongoing self-assessment

Authentic material as input

Theme-based learning linked to task-
based instruction

Attention to all aspects of
communicative competence

GET IT?
GOT IT!

Listening to Others/
Speaking for Ourselves

Mary McVey Gill

Pamela Hartmann

Heinle & Heinle Publishers
A Division of Wadsworth, Inc.
Boston, Massachusetts, 02116, USA

The publication of *Get It? Got It!* was directed by the members of the Heinle & Heinle ESL Publishing Team:

David C. Lee, Editorial Director
Susan Mraz, Marketing Manager
Lisa McLaughlin, Production Editor

Also participating in the publication of this program were:

Publisher: Stanley J. Galek
Editorial Production Manager: Elizabeth Holthaus
Assistant Editor: Kenneth Mattsson
Manufacturing Coordinator: Mary Beth Lynch
Full Service Project Manager/Compositor: Monotype Composition Company
Interior Design: Maureen Lauran
Cover Design: Maureen Lauran

Manufactured in the United States of America.

ISBN: 0-8384-2321-3

Heinle & Heinle Publishers is a division of Wadsworth, Inc.

10 9 8 7 6

Grateful acknowledgment is made for the use of the following:

"Old Country Advice to the American Traveler," from *My Name Is Iran,* Copyright © 1939, renewed 1967 by William Saroyan, reprinted by permission of Harcourt Brace Jovanovich, Inc.

To our mothers,
Bea Hartmann
and
Mary Elizabeth McVey

PHOTO CREDITS

ILLUSTRATIONS

Steven Blank

MAPS

Susan Jones

WELCOME TO TAPESTRY

*E*nter the world of Tapestry! Language learning can be seen as an ever-developing tapestry woven with many threads and colors. The elements of the tapestry are related to different language skills like listening and speaking, reading and writing; the characteristics of the teachers; the desires, needs, and backgrounds of the students; and the general second language development process. When all these elements are working together harmoniously, the result is a colorful, continuously growing tapestry of language competence of which the student and the teacher can be proud.

This volume is part of the Tapestry program for students of English as a second language (ESL) at levels from beginning to "bridge" (which follows the advanced level and prepares students to enter regular postsecondary programs along with native English speakers). Tapestry levels include:

Beginning
Low Intermediate
High Intermediate
Low Advanced
High Advanced
Bridge

Because the Tapestry Program provides a unified theoretical and pedagogical foundation for all its components, you can optimally use all the Tapestry student books in a coordinated fashion as an entire curriculum of materials. (They will be published from 1993 to 1995 with further editions likely thereafter.) Alternatively, you can decide to use just certain Tapestry volumes, depending on your specific needs.

Tapestry is primarily designed for ESL students at postsecondary institutions in North America. Some want to learn ESL for academic or career advancement, others for social and personal reasons. Tapestry builds directly on all these motivations. Tapestry stimulates learners to do their best. It enables learners to use English naturally and to develop fluency as well as accuracy.

Tapestry Principles

The following principles underlie the instruction provided in all of the components of the Tapestry program.

EMPOWERING LEARNERS

Language learners in Tapestry classrooms are active and increasingly responsible for developing their English language skills and related cultural abilities. This self-direction leads to better, more rapid learning. Some cultures virtually train their students to be passive in the classroom, but Tapestry weans them from passivity by providing exceptionally high-interest materials, colorful and motivating activities, personalized self-reflection tasks, peer tutoring and other forms of cooperative learning, and powerful learning strategies to boost self-direction in learning.

The empowerment of learners creates refreshing new roles for teachers, too. The teacher serves as facilitator, co-communicator, diagnostician, guide, and helper. Teachers are set free to be more creative at the same time their students become more autonomous learners.

HELPING STUDENTS IMPROVE THEIR LEARNING STRATEGIES

Learning strategies are the behaviors or steps an individual uses to enhance his or her learning. Examples are taking notes, practicing, finding a conversation partner, analyzing words, using background knowledge, and controlling anxiety. Hundreds of such strategies have been identified. Successful language learners use language learning strategies that are most effective for them given their particular learning style, and they put them together smoothly to fit the needs of a given language task. On the other hand, the learning strategies of less successful learners are a desperate grab-bag of ill-matched techniques.

All learners need to know a wide range of learning strategies. All learners need systematic practice in choosing and applying strategies that are relevant for various learning needs. Tapestry is one of the only ESL programs that overtly weaves a comprehensive set of learning strategies into language activities in all its volumes. These learning strategies are arranged in six broad categories throughout the Tapestry books:

> Forming concepts
> Personalizing
> Remembering new material
> Managing your learning
> Understanding and using emotions
> Overcoming limitations

The most useful strategies are sometimes repeated and flagged with a note, "It Works! Learning Strategy . . ." to remind students to use a learning strategy they have already encountered. This recycling reinforces the value of learning strategies and provides greater practice.

RECOGNIZING AND HANDLING LEARNING STYLES EFFECTIVELY

Learners have different learning styles (for instance, visual, auditory, hands-on; reflective, impulsive; analytic, global; extroverted, introverted; closure-oriented, open). Particularly in an ESL setting, where students come from vastly different cultural backgrounds, learning styles differences abound and can cause "style conflicts."

Unlike most language instruction materials, Tapestry provides exciting activities specifically tailored to the needs of students with a large range of learning styles. You can use any Tapestry volume with the confidence that the activities and materials are intentionally geared for many different styles. Insights from the latest educational and psychological research undergird this style-nourishing variety.

OFFERING AUTHENTIC, MEANINGFUL COMMUNICATION

Students need to encounter language that provides authentic, meaningful communication. They must be involved in real-life communication tasks that cause them to *want* and *need* to read, write, speak, and listen to English. Moreover, the tasks—to be most effective—must be arranged around themes relevant to learners.

Themes like family relationships, survival in the educational system, personal health, friendships in a new country, political changes, and protection of the environment are all valuable to ESL learners. Tapestry focuses on topics like these. In every Tapestry volume, you will see specific content drawn from very broad areas such as home life, science and technology, business, humanities, social sciences, global issues, and multiculturalism. All the themes are real and important, and they are fashioned into language tasks that students enjoy.

At the advanced level, Tapestry also includes special books each focused on a single broad theme. For instance, there are two books on business English, two on English for science and technology, and two on academic communication and study skills.

UNDERSTANDING AND VALUING DIFFERENT CULTURES

Many ESL books and programs focus completely on the "new" culture, that is, the culture which the students are entering. The implicit message is that ESL students should just learn about this target culture, and there is no need to understand their own culture better or to find out about the cultures of their international classmates. To some ESL students, this makes them feel their own culture is not valued in the new country.

Tapestry is designed to provide a clear and understandable entry into North American culture. Nevertheless, the Tapestry Program values *all* the cultures found in the ESL classroom. Tapestry students have constant opportunities to become "culturally fluent" in North American culture while they are learning English, but they also have the chance to think about the cultures of their classmates and even understand their home culture from different perspectives.

INTEGRATING THE LANGUAGE SKILLS

Communication in a language is not restricted to one skill or another. ESL students are typically expected to learn (to a greater or lesser degree) all four language skills: reading, writing, speaking, and listening. They are also expected to develop strong grammatical competence, as well as becoming socioculturally sensitive and knowing what to do when they encounter a "language barrier."

Research shows that multi-skill learning is more effective than isolated-skill learning, because related activities in several skills provide reinforcement and refresh the learner's memory. Therefore, Tapestry integrates all the skills. A given Tapestry volume might highlight one skill, such as reading, but all other skills are also included to support and strengthen overall language development.

However, many intensive ESL programs are divided into classes labeled according to one skill (Reading Comprehension Class) or at most two skills (Listening/Speaking Class or Oral Communication Class). The volumes in the Tapestry Program can easily be used to fit this traditional format, because each volume clearly identifies its highlighted or central skill(s).

Grammar is interwoven into all Tapestry volumes. However, there is also a separate reference book for students, *The Tapestry Grammar,* and a Grammar Strand composed of grammar "work-out" books at each of the levels in the Tapestry Program.

Other Features of the Tapestry Program

PILOT SITES

It is not enough to provide volumes full of appealing tasks and beautiful pictures. Users deserve to know that the materials have been pilot-tested. In many ESL series, pilot testing takes place at only a few sites or even just in the classroom of the author. In contrast, Heine & Heinle Publishers have developed a network of Tapestry Pilot Test Sites throughout North America. At this time, there are approximately 40 such sites, although the number grows weekly. These sites try out the materials and provide suggestions for revisions. They are all actively engaged in making Tapestry the best program possible.

AN OVERALL GUIDEBOOK

To offer coherence to the entire Tapestry Program and especially to offer support for teachers who want to understand the principles and practice of Tapestry, we have written a book entitled, *The Tapestry of Language Learning: The Individual in the Communicative Classroom* (Scarcella and Oxford, published in 1992 by Heinle & Heinle).

A Last Word

We are pleased to welcome you to Tapestry! We use the Tapestry principles every day, and we hope these principles—and all the books in the Tapestry Program—provide you the same strength, confidence, and joy that they give us. We look forward to comments from both teachers and students who use any part of the Tapestry Program.

Rebecca L. Oxford
University of Alabama
Tuscaloosa, Alabama

Robin C. Scarcella
University of California at Irvine
Irvine, California

PREFACE

Get It? Got It! is designed to help connect intermediate ESL students to the real English-speaking world and involve them with authentic language from the beginning. Authentic language should increase students' level of interest and promote a fun class atmosphere. As they listen for main ideas and concepts, students can focus on what they *do* understand, not what they don't understand.

The text covers all four language skills but emphasizes listening and speaking; it can be used as a core text or as a text where listening and speaking are the primary focus.

A wide variety of listening input is provided in different registers. These range from simple conversations and short interviews to radio ads, news stories, songs, and short stories or anecdotes. Some of the material was semi-scripted; this was mainly for the practical competency-based conversations that could not be found already on tape: ordering a meal in a restaurant, calling about a housing ad, or talking to a bus driver. Even these were not fully scripted—people who took the roles were encouraged to improvise. However, most of the material was recorded in the real world.

At first glance, some of the readings and listening passages in this book may seem—to students and teachers alike—to be too difficult. However, the goal is not for students to understand every word. They will find it exciting to find that they can understand much of what they read or listen to *now* and not have to wait for years to graduate from "ESL English" to the real world.

Students develop self-confidence if they can understand the gist of messages that contain unfamiliar words or expressions. They are not expected to understand everything in a listening passage—just enough to complete the task at hand. If they learn to avoid word-for-word translation and develop a tolerance for unfamiliar words, they will soon be able to listen intelligently and grasp key concepts. There are many exercises that encourage students to look at clues to meaning and make intelligent assumptions or predictions. In this way, rather than relying on dictionaries or giving up when there are some unfamiliar words, students should be able to improve their learning strategies and learn English faster.

A note about listening: Listening is one of the most important language skills. Studies show that while people may spend as much as 80 percent of their day in communication, most of the time spent listening is at about a 25 percent efficiency level. In business, it has been estimated that 60 percent of the misunderstandings are due to poor listening. In academic settings, it has been estimated that nearly 90 percent of class time in colleges and high schools in the United States is spent in listening; poor listening skills are a stronger factor in failure in college than poor reading skills or academic aptitude.

Get It? Got It! also practices speaking skills; it encourages students to speak in a variety of situations, both inside and outside the classroom. There are many speaking activities (which occur mostly in the "After You Listen" sections), including role-plays, student-student interviews, polls (inside and outside the class), telephone communication tasks (e.g., calling a business or the INS), discussion (often cross-cultural), problem-solving activities such as making a map or designing an advertising campaign, cooperative learning activities, and so on.

Chapter Features

Language Functions. Many language functions that help students learn speaking skills are covered: expressing opinions, agreeing and disagreeing, apologizing, asking for clarification, opening a conversation, and so on. These functions are essential to develop students' sociolinguistic competence. Where appropriate, there is a box with expressions for the particular function presented.

Grammar Boxes. When a grammar point occurs several times naturally in an authentic listening passage, a grammar box highlighting the structure is included. You can elaborate on these structures if you like. Grammar is treated at greater length in the companion grammar volume of the Tapestry series.

The Sound of It. These optional sections focus on phonological features of the language: reductions, intonation, and stress. See the "Teaching Suggestions" section of this preface or see the instructor's manual for ideas on how to use these sections.

Writing Activities. You can use these or not, depending on what skills you are emphasizing. Writing is covered more fully in the companion writing book of the Tapestry series.

Reading. Short readings are provided to open each chapter, and occasional short readings are offered. In addition, there is a variety of realia (charts, maps, a menu, and so on). However, the focus of the book is not on reading, and if you are using the book as a core text, you may want to bring in additional reading materials. Reading is covered more fully in the companion reading book of the Tapestry series.

Culture. Cross-cultural information and opportunities for discussion are included everywhere throughout the book. Students can bring their own cultures into the classroom and share their background information with others for a student-centered learning experience.

Learning Strategies. Learning strategies are explicitly pointed out to students. For students from a rather traditional, perhaps grammar-translation background of language learning, it's helpful to understand the reasons for the various tasks. Each chapter includes a variety of learning strategies—affective, cognitive, metacognitive, social, and compensation. This is to ensure that students with different learning styles can all benefit to the utmost from the chapter contents. The first time that a learning strategy is presented in the book it is boxed; after that, a marginal indication is used.

Teaching Suggestions

PREVIEW

Almost every chapter opens with a checklist of functions and topics included in the chapter. This gives students a preview of what they'll study. If desired, each student can rank the items in order of importance to him or her. You don't have to collect these, but you might ask students (orally) how many of them chose the first item as number 1, how many the second item, and so on to get a general idea of the students' preferences and perceived needs.

Following this checklist are pictures and short readings to introduce the theme and call up students' background knowledge of the subject. Have the students look at the pictures and tell you what they think the chapter will be about. Then have students answer the prereading questions. Ask any additional prereading questions that you think might interest your class.

Look through each chapter before teaching it to decide what parts you will use and what parts you will skip if there is a lack of time or is one of the materials are less appropriate for your particular class. You might put the topics of the chapter on the board and see which ones are most interesting to the students.

"BEFORE YOU LISTEN"

Each part is divided into three sections: "Before You Listen," "Listening," and "After You Listen." "Before You Listen" contains prelistening activities such as vocabulary work, discussion, scanning a piece of realia, taking a poll, guessing meaning from context, or prediction exercises. Do the "Before You Listen" activities and any additional activities you may want to do to introduce the listening passage. Then proceed to the "Listening" section.

"LISTENING"

Have students read the instructions to the first listening task. Emphasize that they do not need to understand everything in the passage—they simply need to listen for the information required to complete the task. Play the tape all the way through without stopping. Ask students to do the first task, whether it be answering a main idea question, matching pictures to conversations, completing a short form, putting pictures or statements in order, etc. If the students can't complete the task, play the tape all the way through again. In general, if students have trouble with any of the listening passages, provide additional guidance without actually giving them the answers. It's important that students figure out the answers for themselves and feel that they have successfully performed the activity. But don't allow them to become frustrated; instead you can:

1. write some additional key words and expressions on the board before playing the tape again,
2. ask questions to guide students toward the key to understanding the task,
3. stop the tape at a key point or replay a key portion of the tape.

If there is more than one listening task, go on to the second one. Play the tape through again without stopping and proceed as for the first task.

"AFTER YOU LISTEN"

These sections include a wide variety of activities. Do those that are most appropriate to your students' interests and needs and to the goals of the course. You will probably not have time to do all of these for any given chapter.

Some "After You Listen" sections include a survey where students are instructed to ask various people a certain question or questions. Some students may be shy about approaching native English speakers, but try to convince them of the importance of doing this. The first survey includes a section on how to approach someone to ask a question; you might do a role-play to practice this technique. Students might feel more comfortable approaching people who work at your school, who will tend to be helpful. However, you might also want to have students simply work within the class to ask each other questions. In some cases, the survey is intended to elicit cross-cultural responses; the more cultures represented, the more successful the surveys will be. You might want to have students do these in class if the class members are from a variety of cultures.

Many "After You Listen" activities involve pair and group work. For classes in which many languages are represented, encourage students to sit near others who do not speak their language. Then throughout the course, students can easily put themselves in discussion groups in which they won't be tempted to speak their native language. Regularly remind students to encourage everyone in the group to speak. Students need to learn the dynamics of group interaction so that everyone can participate on an equal basis. Tell them that no one should dominate the group and no one should be silent. Change the discussion groups from time to time so that students can experience other cultures, accents, and ideas.

"THE SOUND OF IT"

These phonological sections present information and activities related to reductions, intonation, and stress. After childhood, very few people can learn to mimic sounds of a foreign language in a native-like way. Teaching isolated sounds will probably not do much to improve the pronunciation of your students, but focusing on intonation and stress (in combination with sounds) should help them avoid communication problems due to mispronunciation.

If you live in a region where there are patterns of intonation or pronunciation that differ from those of most of the country, you might point them out to your students. The most common reductions and their spellings are covered here, but there are many ways to reduce words or to spell the reduction. If you prefer another spelling or if there are other reductions that are common in the area in which you live, let your students know.

SELF-EVALUATIONS

Have students complete the forms at the end of the chapter and put them in their portfolios. These forms needn't be shared with other students. The purpose of the evaluations is simply to help the students focus on what they do well and what they need to work on in future chapters. Categories on these forms have been left intentionally broad—e.g., "I understand this pretty well," "I learned something but I need to learn more," "I don't understand this." Culture may play some role in student self-evaluation in that students from some cultures tend to underestimate their performance while students from other cultures might overestimate their performance.

EXTRACURRICULAR LISTENING

Encourage students to watch television in English from the beginning of the course with the goal of improving their listening comprehension. Although the TV news is not specifically covered until Chapter 9, it would probably be best to introduce TV news early in the term. (See Chapter 9, Part Two, Activity B.) This can be one of the most rewarding and beneficial activities that students can do. Although at first students will probably complain that they can't understand the news, don't let them give up. Tell them that it's all right if they understand just a few words in the beginning because many words will appear again and again on the news, and their vocabulary will increase rapidly. In addition, there is tremendous benefit to this activity because it enables students to keep in touch with world events, including events in their own countries. If there is a weekly small-group discussion, this becomes a wonderfully dynamic interactive task in which students share news items with each other and build on what each student has said. Although skeptical at first, students will soon develop a sense of self-confidence and will be excited that they can understand more than they had ever thought possible because they are focusing on main ideas and not on individual troublesome vocabulary items. If you begin this activity early in the term, you can use these instructions (or similar instructions), perhaps adding them to the form in Chapter 9:

> Directions: As part of your work in this class, you'll need to watch one-half hour of news on TV every night and make notes on this form. At first this might seem difficult, but it does get easier! In the beginning, you might understand just a few words. But you'll understand more and more each time. *Don't give up.* (Nothing gets easier if you give up.)

ASSESSMENT

If you use a variety of assessment measurements, you will probably be fairest to your students, who may have different learning styles, needs, and interests. One of the best ways to assess students is to have them keep a portfolio of their work. In many cases, this text instructs students to put something in their portfolios: a writing assignment, a form they have filled out, survey results, a conversation they have performed on a tape, and so on. The portfolios can include the students' answers to the opening needs/interests questionnaire in each chapter and peer responses to their assignments as well as your own evaluations. Self-evaluations are provided at the end of each chapter and will help students work toward their goals. Many teachers will also want to use oral interviews with their students, grade according to class participation, assess their work in a pair or group activity, or use the vocabulary activities provided in the instructor's manual as short quizzes.

Instructor's Manual/Tapescript

The instructor's manual includes the tapescript, instructions for how to use a sample chapter, chapter-by-chapter notes, a list of vocabulary featured in each chapter, and vocabulary activities. The latter can be used to teach vocabulary or for testing purposes.

Acknowledgments

The authors would like to thank Rebecca Oxford and Robin Scarcella for the pioneering of the Tapestry program and for their good cheer throughout the project. We are also very grateful to the following people at Heinle & Heinle for their support and help: our editorial director, David Lee, who with Rebecca and Robin initiated the series; assistant editor Ken Mattsson; recording supervisor Tab Hamlin; and production editor Lisa McLaughlin. Our sincere appreciation to Vee Sawyer and John Budz of Monotype Composition for their hard work in meeting a very difficult schedule. We would also like to thank Nina Liakos (University of Maryland), Sibyl Senters (Language Studies International, Boston), and Linda Swanson (U.S. International University) for their helpful comments during the development of this manuscript. Also thanks to Della Gilchrist (California State University, Los Angeles) and her students for testing the material in the classroom.

We would like to thank the following people for lending their voices and ideas to the tape recordings: Heidelinda de Lapp, Richard Echternach, Margie Hutton, Joanne Press, Edward Schwarz, Zaman Stanizai, Tim Wahl, Florene Rozen, and Dorothy Washington. A special thank you to William Logan for his recording of "Sometimes I Feel Like a Motherless Child." Finally, a very affectionate thanks to Bea Hartmann, Mary Elizabeth and Richard McVey, and John Gill for their help in finding materials and for their constant support.

Mary McVey Gill	Pamela Hartmann
Stanford, California	Evans Community Adult School
	Los Angeles, California

CONTENTS

3 This Is Who I Am   39

PREVIEW

4 Health: Getting the Most out of Life   57

PREVIEW

8 Advertising . . . and Shopping 127

PREVIEW

9 What's in the News 149

PREVIEW

On the Move

Millions of American immigrants passed through Ellis Island, near New York City, on their way to a new life. Says writer Jonathan Raban: "On the way from Europe, they'd lost their names, families, occupations, uniforms, languages." When they arrived in America, he says, they had a new choice: Who did they want to become?

—*Jonathan Raban, Hunting Mr. Heartbreak (London: Collins Harvill, 1990), p. 61.*

Look at the pictures and read the information.

"The United States has one of the most mobile populations in the world. The average American moves more than ten times during his life. This year alone more than 40 million of us—roughly one in six—will change addresses, and it will cost us more than $5 billion." The truck in the picture belongs to the U-Haul company, which for many years had a saying, "Make Moving an Adventure."

Patricia Skalka, "Reader's Digest Guide to Moving" (New York: *Reader's Digest*, March 1989), p. M1.

"My family moved from one town to another in eastern North Carolina, and I loved every move. . . . I am still on the move. . . . I keep thinking I'll find something wonderful just around the next bend. And I always do."

Charles Kuralt, "What I Learned on the Road," from *A Life on the Road* (New York: *Reader's Digest*, March 1991), p. 99.

QUESTIONS

1. How many times does the average American move in his or her life?
2. How many Americans will move this year?

LEARNING STRATEGY

Understanding and Using Emotions: Talking about your feelings helps you better understand yourself and others.

DISCUSSION

1. Jonathan Raban says that Americans can move to any state or country—they can still speak English, watch the TV shows they watched at home, and eat at Burger King restaurants. This is true all over the United States, he says, and all over the world. Is it easier for a person from your country to live in the United States or Canada or for an American or Canadian to live in your country? Why?

2. Yakov Smirnoff, a comedian, came to the United States from Russia and is now an American citizen. He says, "You can go to England, but you can't become an Englishman. You can go to France, but you can't become a Frenchman. But you can come to America and become an American." Do you agree? Can you come to America and *become an American*? Give examples to show your point of view.

PART ONE: CALLING ABOUT A HOUSING AD

Before You Listen

A. Susan Evans is one of 40 million Americans who are moving this year. She is looking for an apartment in San Francisco, California. She sees an ad in the newspaper:

Look at the ad and answer these questions.

One bdrm. apt. for rent.
Nice area. Good transportation.
Call 555~1616.

1. What questions will Susan probably ask the apartment manager? Work with a partner and make a list.
2. What questions will the apartment manager probably ask Susan? Work with a partner and make a list.

SUSAN'S QUESTIONS	APARTMENT MANAGER'S QUESTIONS
_____	_____
_____	_____
_____	_____
_____	_____

4

Forming Concepts: By guessing the meanings of new words, you improve your vocabulary without constantly using the dictionary.

Threads

The United States has a true love affair with the automobile: it has more than three times as many vehicles as Japan, with the second largest number of cars.

B. In Conversation 1, Susan is talking to an apartment manager. Before you listen, guess the meanings of the <u>underlined</u> words in the sentences below.

1. I need an apartment soon. The one on Elm Street won't be <u>available</u> for six weeks, but the one on Post Street is ready now. I'm going to look at the apartment on Post Street today.
2. The rent includes <u>utilities</u>, like gas and electricity.
3. I have to pay a <u>security deposit</u> of $300 when I move into my new apartment. I'm going to leave the place in good condition. Then I can get my $300 back when I move out.
4. I also have to pay <u>first and last month's rent</u>. That is, I have to pay two months' rent before I move in.
5. I have two <u>pets</u>: a dog and a cat.
6. I live on Mayfield Avenue. The <u>cross street</u> is San Rafael Way. My apartment isn't on the corner of Mayfield and San Rafael, but it's very close.

Listening

A. Susan calls about the apartment. Listen to Conversation 1. As you listen, look at your list of questions. Which questions does Susan ask? Which questions does the apartment manager ask? Check (✓) them on your list on page 3.

B. Listen again. Answer these questions. You may have to listen several times.
1. Look at your list of questions. Does Susan ask other questions that aren't on your list? Does the apartment manager ask questions that aren't on your list? Add any new questions to your list.
2. What is Susan going to do in an hour?

After You Listen

2 BEDROOM APT. Large kitchen. New carpets and paint. 2550 Parkwood Ave. 555-1029

Look at the housing ad. Write three questions that you would ask about the apartment.

1. _____
2. _____
3. _____

PART TWO: USING PUBLIC TRANSPORTATION; ASKING FOR AND UNDERSTANDING DIRECTIONS

Before You Listen

LEARNING STRATEGY

Remembering New Material: To remember vocabulary, associate new words with words you already know.

Susan goes to the apartment. On her way, she talks to two different bus drivers. For each expression on the left, tell which expression on the right has the same meaning. Write the letter on the line.

___b___ **1.** Excuse me.   **a.** paper money

_____ **2.** to transfer   **b.** Pardon me.

_____ **3.** dollar bills   **c.** correct amount in coins

_____ **4.** exact change   **d.** to change

LEARNING STRATEGY

Forming Concepts: Listen to people's tone of voice, because sometimes tones tell more than words.

Listening

A. Susan has two conversations on her way to the apartment, with two different bus drivers. Listen to Conversations 1 and 2. One of the drivers is friendly, and one is unfriendly.
Which driver is friendly?

_____ **1.** the driver in Conversation 1

_____ **2.** the driver in Conversation 2

> ## CULTURE NOTE
>
> It's not very polite to call a woman lady. Miss is much more polite. Ma'am is for older women. Remember that Americans want to be young more than they want respect. You can call a man sir, but it's not polite to call a man mister without his last name.

5

B. Listen to Conversations 1 and 2 again. Answer these questions. Check (✓) the correct answers. You may need to listen several times.

CONVERSATION 1

1. Which buses does Susan need to take to Seventh and Lake Streets?

_____ **a.** the 13 and the 30

_____ **b.** the 30 and the 38

2. Where does she transfer?

_____ **a.** at Geary Street

_____ **b.** at Lake Street

CONVERSATION 2

1. How much does it cost to take the bus?

_____ **a.** 85 cents

_____ **b.** one dollar and 85 cents

2. What does Susan need?

_____ **a.** exact change

_____ **b.** a dollar bill

After You Listen

LEARNING STRATEGY

Overcoming Limitations: Role-playing helps prepare you for regular conversation.

A. Work with a partner. Student A wants to take the bus. Student B is a bus driver. Have a conversation. Follow this model:

STUDENT A: Excuse me. Does this bus go to. . . ?
STUDENT B: No, . . . You need bus number. . . .
STUDENT A: Where do I get . . . ?
STUDENT B: . . .
STUDENT A: How much . . . ?
STUDENT B: . . .
STUDENT A: Thanks.

B. After you finish, write your conversation. Your teacher may want you to present it to the class or put it on tape. Put it in your portfolio.

Threads

Many Americans do not want to take public transportation or share rides to work because the drive to work in their cars is their only quiet time alone.

Before You Listen

Remembering New Material: Identifying things in a picture helps you remember vocabulary.

Susan arrives at the apartment. Work in small groups. Before you listen, fill in this plan of an American home. Write the names of the rooms inside the plan and the names of the other things outside the plan. Use these lists:

ROOMS/AREAS OF A HOUSE

kitchen	bedroom (2)	
dining room	living room	
bathroom	hallway	

THINGS IN A HOUSE

refrigerator	bed	sofa	table and chairs
stove	closet	bathtub	lamp
dishwasher	toilet	coffee table	chest of drawers

chest of drawers

hallway

Listening

A. Susan arrives at 1515 Seventh Avenue. Listen to the conversation. How many rooms of a house do you hear? Check them on the list on page 7. Note: The apartment is not the same as the picture of the typical home on page 7.

LEARNING STRATEGY

Remembering New Material: Putting items into groups (for example, good things and bad things) helps you remember them.

B. Listen to the conversation again. Write as many good and bad things about the apartment as possible. You may have to listen several times.

GOOD THINGS ABOUT THE APARTMENT	BAD THINGS ABOUT THE APARTMENT
quiet	_unfurnished (no furniture)_

After You Listen

LEARNING STRATEGY

Remembering New Material: Practicing conversations can strengthen your memory.

A. Work with a partner. Look at the conversation below. One student is A, and one student is B. Take roles and have a conversation. Choose words from the lists. Then change roles and have another conversation. Choose different words from the lists.

A: Oh, what a $\begin{Bmatrix} \text{big} \\ \text{sunny} \\ \text{lovely} \end{Bmatrix}$ apartment!

B: Yes, it $\begin{Bmatrix} \text{is beautiful.} \\ \text{is large.} \\ \text{gets a lot of light.} \end{Bmatrix}$

A: What a nice, clean kitchen! The $\begin{Bmatrix} \text{oven} \\ \text{stove} \\ \text{refrigerator} \end{Bmatrix}$ looks new.

B: Right! And there's also a $\begin{Bmatrix} \text{lot of storage space.} \\ \text{garbage disposal.} \\ \text{dishwasher.} \end{Bmatrix}$

A: Is there a $\begin{Bmatrix} \text{garage?} \\ \text{swimming pool?} \\ \text{security guard?} \end{Bmatrix}$

B: Yes, and there's $\begin{Bmatrix} \text{a tennis court} \\ \text{a recreation area} \\ \text{cable television} \end{Bmatrix}$ too.

A: Is there a $\begin{Bmatrix} \text{school} \\ \text{library} \\ \text{park} \end{Bmatrix}$ nearby?

B: Of course, and there's a $\begin{Bmatrix} \text{bus stop} \\ \text{grocery store} \\ \text{hospital} \end{Bmatrix}$ right down the street.

A: I hope there's $\begin{Bmatrix} \text{a fireplace.} \\ \text{air conditioning.} \\ \text{a good view.} \end{Bmatrix}$

B: There is!

A: This is a $\begin{Bmatrix} \text{great} \\ \text{terrific} \\ \text{wonderful} \end{Bmatrix}$ apartment! How much is the rent?

B: Only $1500 a month.

A: $1500 a month! Oh, no!

B. Work with a partner. Look at the housing ads in your local newspaper. Choose an ad for an apartment. Have a conversation about the ad. One student is the apartment manager, and the other student is looking for an apartment. The person looking for an apartment calls the apartment manager to ask questions. Don't forget to ask about utilities, things in the area (such as grocery stores or banks), the cross street, and so on. The apartment manager also asks a few questions.

C. After you finish, write your conversation. Your teacher may want you to present it to the class or put in on tape. Put it in your portfolio.

LEARNING STRATEGY

Personalizing: Sometimes you can dream about ideal (perfect) things . . . just for fun.

D. Do you have a "dream house"? That is, what would the ideal house or apartment for you be like? Write a short description of it. Share the description with a classmate and then put it in your portfolio.

PART FOUR: ASKING, UNDERSTANDING, AND GIVING DIRECTIONS

Before You Listen

Susan decides to take the apartment. She moves in one week later. Her neighbor, Takeshi Matsui, is a very nice student at the local college. Susan asks him questions about where to find things in the neighborhood. Look at the map on page 11.

Here are some things Takeshi tells her.

1. The post office is **across the street from** the bank.
2. The bakery is **down the street from** the post office.
3. The laundromat is **next to (beside)** the grocery store.
4. The drugstore is **around the corner from** the laundromat.
5. There's a bus stop **in front of** the library.
6. There's a parking lot **behind (in back of)** the department store.

Listening

Takeshi tells Susan where to find things that she needs. Look at the map again. Listen and complete the sentences. Check the correct answers.

IT WORKS!
Learning Strategy:
Identifying

1. _____ **a.** bookstore
   _____ **b.** park
   _____ **c.** laundromat

2. _____ **a.** bookstore
   _____ **b.** park
   _____ **c.** drugstore

3. _____ **a.** bank
   _____ **b.** grocery store
   _____ **c.** Chinese restaurant

4. _____ **a.** post office
   _____ **b.** laundromat
   _____ **c.** bookstore

5. _____ **a.** department store
   _____ **b.** park
   _____ **c.** bakery

6. _____ **a.** library
   _____ **b.** bakery
   _____ **c.** drugstore

After You Listen

A. Work in groups and make a map. One person is the map maker. The others give directions. Make a simple map of the area around your school. Include stores, banks, and so on. Don't point to the map. *Tell* the map maker where to put each thing. Use these expressions: *across the street from, down the street from, next to, beside, around the corner from, in front of, in back of, behind.*

> **EXAMPLES**: Kim's Market is in front of the school, on Main Street. There's a Chinese restaurant around the corner from the school, on Fifth and Main.

B. Play a guessing game. Look at the map your group made for Exercise A. One person in the group chooses a place. He or she gives directions from the school to that place. The others try to guess the name of the place. Use these expressions:

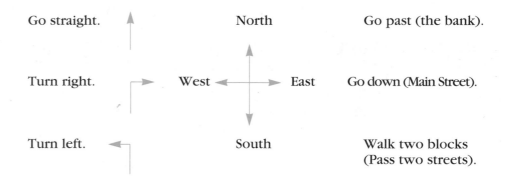

Go straight.   North   Go past (the bank).

Turn right.   West   East   Go down (Main Street).

Turn left.   South   Walk two blocks (Pass two streets).

> **EXAMPLE**:   **STUDENT A:** Go out of the school onto First Street and turn left. Walk two blocks. Turn right. Pass the library. It's on your left.
>   **STUDENT B:** Lincoln Park?
>   **STUDENT A:** Yes!

C. Work with a partner. Student A looks at Map A of San Francisco, on page 13. Student B looks at Map B of San Francisco on page 14. Under each map is a list of places. Ask your partner how to get to each place on the list under your map. Your partner will give you directions. Begin each time from Market and Powell, where the cable car line starts. Listen to your partner, then write the name of the place by one of the question marks (?) on your map. Then your partner will ask you how to get to one of the places on the list under his or her map. Find the place on your map and give your partner directions. Remember to start from Market and Powell. Take turns.

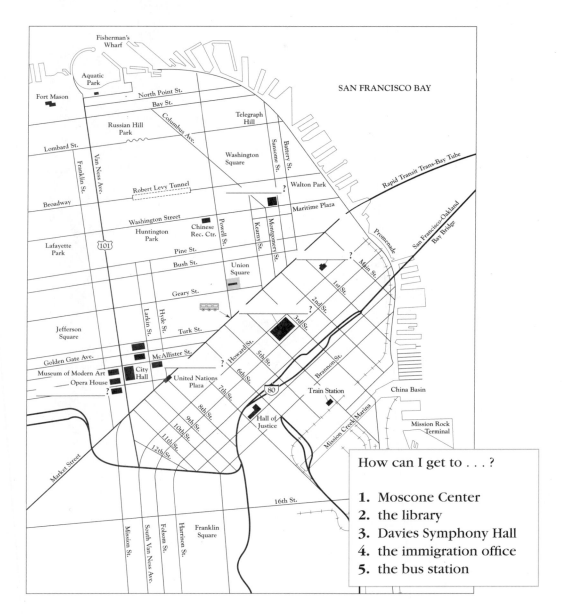

How can I get to . . . ?

1. Moscone Center
2. the library
3. Davies Symphony Hall
4. the immigration office
5. the bus station

ASKING DIRECTIONS

How do you get to . . . ?

Could you tell me where . . . is?

Is . . . far from here?

I'm looking for . . . .

I'm trying to find . . . .

In what direction is . . . ?

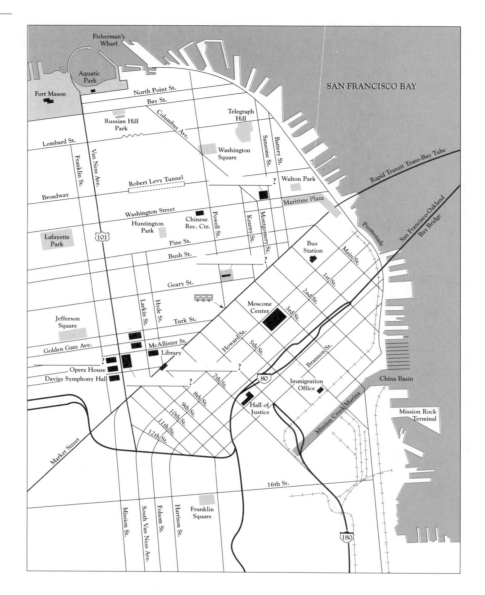

How can I get to . . . ?

1. city hall
2. the United Nations Plaza
3. Union Square
4. the train station
5. the museum of modern art

Forming Concepts: Taking a poll (interviewing or talking to other people about a specific topic) gives you new ideas and information.

E. Talk to three classmates, people at your school, or people in your community. Ask them where to find each of these things. Complete the chart with their answers. *information*
Excuse me. (Hello there.) I'm taking a poll for my English class. May I ask you a quick question?

GETTING SOMEONE'S ATTENTION

	PERSON 1	PERSON 2	PERSON 3
1. a good Chinese restaurant	_____	_____	_____
2. a good Mexican restaurant	_____	_____	_____
3. a good _____ (you fill in) restaurant	_____	_____	_____
4. a movie theater	_____	_____	_____
5. an inexpensive supermarket	_____	_____	_____
6. a good drugstore	_____	_____	_____
7. a nice park	_____	_____	_____
8. a great place to go on weekends	_____	_____	_____

The Sound of It: Understanding Reductions

A. In normal or fast speech, you will hear "reductions" of some words. For instance, *want to* may sound like "wanna." Learning to understand reductions will help you become a better listener. Listen to these examples of reductions from the conversations in this chapter. Can you hear the difference between the long forms and the short forms?

LONG FORM	REDUCTION	SHORT FORM
Do you have any pets?	you → ya*	Do ya* have any pets?
What's your name?	what's your → whatcher*	Whatcher* name?
Does this bus go to Geary Street?	to → ta*	Does this bus go ta* Geary Street?
Do you want to see the kitchen?	want to → wanna*	Do you wanna* see the kitchen?
You have to have exact change.	have to → hafta*	You hafta* have exact change.

These forms are not correct in writing.

16

Forming Concepts: Analyzing new information helps you understand it better.

B. Listen to these sentences. Do you hear a reduction? Check *Long Form* or *Short Form* as you listen.

	LONG FORM	SHORT FORM
Examples:		
a. <u>You</u> need bus number 3.	X	
b. <u>You</u> need bus number 3.		X
1. Are <u>you</u> Susan Evans?		
2. <u>You</u> can't use dollar bills.		
3. <u>What's your</u> phone number?		
4. <u>What's your</u> address?		
5. <u>I'm</u> here <u>to</u> see the apartment.		
6. Are you going <u>to</u> Parkwood Avenue?		
7. Does he <u>want to</u> pay that much?		
8. I don't <u>want to</u> walk.		
9. Do you <u>have to</u> go?		
10. I <u>have to</u> buy some furniture.		

PART FIVE: A NATION ON THE MOVE

Before You Listen

Forming Concepts: Remember to use guessing as a means of understanding.

A. Guess the meanings of the underlined words in the sentences below.
  1. In the United States, the Congress makes laws. The Congress is the <u>House of Representatives</u> and the Senate.
  2. The number of representatives a state sends to the House of Representatives depends on its <u>population</u>, or the number of people it has.
  3. Each representative has a seat or position in the House—a <u>House seat</u>.
  4. An increase, or <u>gain</u>, in representatives means that a state has more people.
  5. A decrease, or <u>loss</u>, in representatives means that a state has fewer people.
  6. You can talk to people (or write to them) to get information or opinions. This is called taking a poll. People answer a question and someone writes the results. A <u>census</u> is a poll to find out how many people there are in a certain area and perhaps other information about the population.

B. For each expression on the left, tell which expression on the right has the same meaning. Write the letter on the line.

  _g_ **1.** country(side)   **a.** half

  _____ **2.** 50 percent   **b.** employment

  _____ **3.** job   **c.** representative

  _____ **4.** poll   **d.** increase

  _____ **5.** House member   **e.** census

  _____ **6.** gain   **f.** decrease

  _____ **7.** loss   **g.** rural

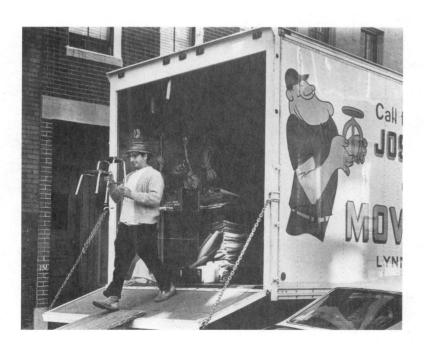

Forming Concepts: Use pictures and charts to understand words.

C. Look at the picture and answer these questions.
1. What areas had more people in 1990 than in 1980?
2. What areas had fewer people in 1990 than in 1980?
3. What city in the United States has the largest population?

A Nation on the Move

The 1990 Census shows how Americans chased dreams and ran from nightmares, trading inland areas for sunny—and increasingly crowded—coastal states

Central
Parts of the Midwest were hit hard: because of their declining populations, Illinois, Michigan and Ohio will each lose two House seats, and four states along the Mississippi will lose a total of five.

Northeast
The New York City area remains the nation's main megalopos, with more than 18 million people. But New York State will lose three House seats.

California
Now home to 29.8 million people, the state has 65% more residents than runner-up New York, and a record total of 52 House seats.

Texas
Over the past decade Texas grew 20%, to 17 million people. Now the third most populous state in the nation, Texas will gain an additional three House seats.

Florida
The nation's fourth most populous state, it now boasts 13 million people. Having grown 33% during the 1980s, the Sunshine State has gained an additional four House seats.

Source: Time magazine, April 29, 1991, p. 30.

Listening

Listen to "A Nation on the Move" and answer these questions.

1. Why did many people move to California, Texas, and Florida in the 1980s?
2. Do more people in the United States live in big cities or rural areas?

After You Listen

A. Interview five or six people from your class or school, including the teacher. Find out how often they and their families have moved. Write their answers in the chart.

NAME	TIMES THEY HAVE MOVED IN THEIR LIFETIME			TIMES THEIR PARENTS HAVE MOVED IN THEIR LIFETIME		
	1-3	4-6	7-10	1-3	4-6	7-10
_____	____	____	____	____	____	____
_____	____	____	____	____	____	____
_____	____	____	____	____	____	____
_____	____	____	____	____	____	____
_____	____	____	____	____	____	____
_____	____	____	____	____	____	____

Threads

More than half of all Americans who move to new states move to Florida, California, Arizona, and Texas.

QUESTIONS

1. Do your classmates move often?
2. Do your classmates' parents move often? How do they compare to the average American? (The average American moves ten times in his or her lifetime.)

CULTURE NOTE

Did you know that the "average" American:

- has at least one pet
- lives in a household of three people
- spends 1/3 of his or her money on housing
- lives within 50 miles of a coastline

LEARNING STRATEGY

Forming Concepts: Listening to music helps you understand another culture, even if you don't understand all the words to the song.

B. The history of the United States is a history of movement, mainly toward the west. Listen to these songs. The first one, "O California," is about the people who went to California looking for gold in 1849. It is similar to the famous song "Oh, Susanna," by Stephen Foster and makes fun of people who thought they would get rich in California. (Most people did not find gold there.) The second one, "Lake Wobegon," is from a popular radio show. Garrison Keillor, the host of the show, moved away from a small town in the middle of the United States, a town he calls "Lake Wobegon." Can you guess why many Americans identify with and like this show? Listen to the songs for fun. You don't need to understand all the words.

O, California

I sailed from Salem City with my washbowl on my knee.
I'm going to California, the gold dust for to see.
It rained all night the day I left, the weather it was dry;
The sun so hot I froze to death, oh brothers don't you cry.
Oh, California, that's the land for me.
I'm going to San Francisco with my washbowl on my knee.
I soon shall be in Frisco, and there I'll look around.
And when I find the gold lumps there, I'll pick them off the ground.
I'll scrape the mountains clean, my boys, I'll drain the rivers dry;
A pocketful of rocks bring home, oh brothers don't you cry.
O, California, that's the land for me.
I'm going to San Francisco with my washbowl on my knee.

WEM Records, Kent McNeil, "Moving West."

Lake Wobegon

Skies were blue; my eyes were too
When I lived in Lake Wobegon
Long ago and now I know
Joy was mine in my prairie home.

Wheat fields in the month of May,
Wheat beside the long driveway;
Now I buy a box of biscuits
Remind me of my Wobegon days.

Folks were warm home on the farm.
Food was good; my clothes were mended.
Then one day, cold and gray,
I packed a grip and moved away.

I looked back and shed a tear
To see it in the rearview mirror.
I said I'd just be gone a couple months,
And now it's almost fifteen years.

Oh, little town, I love the sound
Of water sprinklers in the evening,
The siren tune at 12:00 o'clock noon
Or 12:04 if Bud is late.

And when you walk down Oak or Main
Everybody knows your name.
They ask you how you are;
You say, "Not bad. All right. I guess about the same."

Wobegon, I remember oh so well
How peacefully among the woods and fields you lie.
I won't lie: I close my eyes and I can see you
just as clearly as in days gone by.

LEARNING STRATEGY

Managing Your Learning: Evaluate your own progress so you can become a better learner.

SELF-EVALUATION

Here is a list of some things that you studied in this chapter. How did you do on each item? Check your answers.

	I UNDERSTAND THIS PRETTY WELL	I LEARNED SOMETHING BUT I NEED TO LEARN MORE	I DON'T UNDERSTAND THIS
I studied:			
how to call about housing ads	____	____	____
how to use public transportation	____	____	____
how to ask, understand, and give directions	____	____	____
how to talk to landlords or apartment managers	____	____	____
how to understand people when they speak fast	____	____	____
about how often and where Americans move	____	____	____

What's one thing that you would like to improve about your listening or speaking in the next chapter?

I'm going to work on . . .

_____

_____

_____

_____

_____

The Whole World Is Your Classroom

CHAPTER 2

*T*his chapter has three parts. You'll find out how to improve your English outside the classroom, and you'll practice starting conversations, making small talk, and ending conversations. Look at this list of some of the things that you'll study in this chapter. What's most important for you to learn? Put a 1. What's next most important? Put a 2, etc.

I WANT TO LEARN:

A. **some good things to do to learn a language** _____

B. **how to begin a conversation** _____

C. **how to make small talk** _____

D. **how to understand intonation in tag questions (like *didn't he?*)** _____

E. **how to introduce someone** _____

F. **how to say that I'm sorry** _____

G. **how to express thanks** _____

H. **how to end a conversation** _____

Look at the picture and answer the questions.
1. What are the people in the picture doing?
2. What might they be talking about?

IT WORKS!
Learning Strategy:
Making Predictions

OUR DINNER TABLE UNIVERSITY

When Papa was growing up at the turn of the century in a village in northern Italy, education was for the rich. Papa was the son of a dirt-poor farmer. He used to tell us that he couldn't recall a single day when he wasn't working. He was taken from school in the fifth grade and went to work in a factory.

The world became his school. He was interested in everything. He read all the books, magazines, and newspapers he could lay his hands on. He loved to listen to the town elders and learn about the world beyond this tiny region that was home to generations of Buscaglias before him.

Papa insisted that we learn at least one new thing each day. And dinner seemed the perfect time for sharing what we had learned that day. Naturally, as children, we thought this was crazy.

When my brother and sisters and I got together in the bathroom to clean up for dinner, the question was: "What did *you* learn today?" If the answer was "Nothing," we did not dare sit at the table without first finding a fact in our much-used encyclopedia. "The population of Nepal is . . ."

Now, with our fact, we were ready for dinner. I can still see the table, with mountains of pasta so large that I was often unable to see my sister sitting across the table from me.

Dinner was a noisy time of clattering dishes and conversations, conducted in an Italian dialect since Mama didn't speak English.

Then came the time to share the day's new learning. Papa, at the head of the table, would push back his chair, pour a glass of red wine, light up a cigar, and inhale deeply.

Finally, his attention would settle on one of us. "Felice," he'd say, "tell me what you learned today."

"I learned the population of Nepal is . . ."

Silence.

First, Papa would think about it. "The population of Nepal. Hmmm. Well."

He would then look down the table at Mama, fixing her favorite fruit in a bit of leftover wine. "Mama, did you know that?"

"Nepal?" she'd say. "I don't even know where in God's world it is!"

"Felice," Papa would say. "Get the atlas so we can show Mama where Nepal is." And the whole family went on a search for Nepal.

This same experience was repeated until each family member had a turn. No dinner ended without at least half a dozen such facts.

Papa's technique has served me well all my life. Now before my head hits the pillow each night, I hear Papa's voice: "Felice, what did you learn today?"

Adapted from *Papa, My Father,* by Leo Buscaglia Ph.D. Copyright 1989, by Leo F. Buscaglia, Inc. Published by Slack, Inc.

QUESTIONS

1. When did Leo ("Felice") Buscaglia's father leave school? Where did he get his education?
2. What did each Buscaglia child need to do at the dinner table every night?

LEARNING STRATEGY

Personalizing: Talking with other students about your past experiences helps you better understand yourself and others and also increases your language ability.

DISCUSSION

1. What did you usually talk about at dinner time when you were a child?
2. What do you remember most about your mother or father? What was the most important thing you learned from them?

Before You Listen

IT WORKS!
Learning Strategy:
Identifying

A. How can you learn English *fast*?

 1. Read this list of activities. Number them in order of importance. (What do you think is most important? Put a 1 on that line. What's next? Put a 2, and so on.) Some of these activities are not good. Which ones? Put an X on the lines.

 _____ Come to class every day.

 _____ Ask the teacher when you don't understand something.

 _____ When you read, look up every new word (in a dictionary) and translate it.

 _____ Make friends with people who don't speak your language.

 _____ Watch one-half hour of news on TV every night.

 _____ Speak English with native speakers whenever possible— for example, with someone at a supermarket.

 _____ When you read, *don't* look up every new word. Try to guess the meaning instead.

 _____ Go to movies that are in your new language.

 _____ Keep a list of new words that are important to you.

 _____ Talk with other students in English during class breaks.

 _____ Take a class (in English) in art, music, computers, or something else that interests you.

 _____ Don't say anything in English if the grammar isn't correct.

 _____ Don't be afraid to make mistakes.

 2. Compare your list with another student's list. Are your ideas similar or different? Which activities did you say were not good?

 3. Ask your teacher for his or her ideas. Which activities does your teacher say are not good?

IT WORKS!
Learning Strategy:
Guessing

B. You are going to hear a teacher talking about learning English. Before you listen, guess the meanings of the underlined words in the sentences below.

 1. The doctor gave me these <u>pills</u>. I have to take one pill in the morning and another at night. He says I'll feel better soon.

 2. We didn't talk about anything important. We just <u>made small talk</u> about the weather.

 3. We need some fresh fruit and vegetables, so I'll go over to the <u>produce</u> section while you get the meat.

 4. He looks so happy! He's <u>grinning from ear to ear</u>. I've never seen such a big smile on his face before!

 5. She's been planning this trip for a long time. Now she finds out that she can't go. She's very <u>disappointed</u>. She wanted to go.

Threads

You're never too old to learn.

Proverb

26

Listening

Forming Concepts: If you listen for the main ideas, you understand more effectively.

SECTION 1

You will hear a teacher talk about how to learn English fast. Listen once. Then answer this question:

Who is the best teacher, according to the speaker?

_____ **1.** a strict teacher who gives a lot of homework and does all of the talking

_____ **2.** a friendly teacher who lets the students talk a lot

_____ **3.** you, the learner

SECTION 2

The teacher gives a lot of examples of how to practice English outside of class. What examples does she give? Listen once and check (✓) the answers.

_____ **1.** supermarket   _____ **3.** hospital   _____ **5.** library

_____ **2.** movie theater   _____ **4.** bus stop   _____ **6.** school

SECTION 3

The teacher talks about her friend Sara. What four things did Sara do to learn English? Listen once and check the answers.

_____ **1.** talked with people everywhere

_____ **2.** took a class in English as a second language

_____ **3.** asked friends for help

_____ **4.** listened carefully

_____ **5.** wrote idioms in a notebook

SECTION 4

The teacher talks about her own experience. With whom did she practice a lot of Greek? Listen once and check the best answer.

_____ **1.** her Greek teacher

_____ **2.** taxi drivers

_____ **3.** friends

_____ **4.** neighbors

After You Listen

LEARNING STRATEGY

Forming Concepts: Brainstorming—rapidly discussing and listing ideas related to a main topic—helps you make mental connections.

Work with a small group (three to four students). Choose one person to be the group's "secretary." Brainstorm answers to the following questions:

Where can you make small talk in English in your city?
With whom can you speak English?

Think of all the possibilities. Your secretary will write the list.

Threads

Education is discipline for the adventure of life.

Alfred North Whitehead

Before You Listen

A. Work with a partner. Look at the pictures below. Where does each picture take place (happen)?

☐

_____

_____

_____

☐

_____

_____

☐

_____

_____

_____

☐

B. The people in the pictures don't know each other. They're making small talk. What are they saying? (Make guesses.) With your partner, write a very short conversation (at least two sentences) under each picture.

_____

_____

_____

29

Listening

A. You will hear four short conversations. Look at the pictures on page 29. Which conversation goes with each picture? Listen and write the number (1, 2, 3, or 4) in the box next to the appropriate picture.

B. Listen again to the first sentence of each conversation. Choose a response (answer). Write the number of the conversation (1, 2, 3, or 4) on the line.

_____ It was terrible! I don't think I did very well.

_____ Thanks. She's pretty happy most of the time.

_____ Yeah. And the music's wonderful.

_____ It sure seems to be. Honestly, this bus is late *so* often!

After You Listen

A. How do people *politely* begin a conversation with a stranger? Does it depend on their culture? Ask students from different countries about the questions on the chart below. Then ask your teacher about the United States. Put checkmarks in the boxes.
Example: In your country, is it okay to say to a stranger, "It's hot today, isn't it?"

IT WORKS!
Learning Strategy:
Developing Cultural
Understanding

B. Work in groups. Discuss the answers from your poll. What countries or cultures have the same customs for beginning a conversation? Which ones have different customs? Are there customs in some countries that are not appropriate in the United States?

Situation	First sentence in a conversation with a stranger	Country #1: _____	Country #2: _____	Country #3: _____	Country #4: _____	Country #5: _____ The U.S.
at the bus stop	It's hot today, isn't it?	_____	_____	_____	_____	_____
at the post office	This line is really slow, isn't it?	_____	_____	_____	_____	_____
at a party	You have beautiful eyes. Are you married?	_____	_____	_____	_____	_____
in a supermarket	These tomatoes look terrible, don't they?	_____	_____	_____	_____	_____
on a bus	You're a foreigner, aren't you?	_____	_____	_____	_____	_____
anywhere	I want to practice English with you.	_____	_____	_____	_____	_____
in a museum	This is a wonderful painting, isn't it?	_____	_____	_____	_____	_____

C. Work with a partner. Choose two of the pictures below. Pretend you are in the situations. Make polite small talk for as long as possible.

D. Choose one of the conversations that you've just had. (You and your partner should agree on which one.) Write it out. Your teacher may ask you to put it on tape. Put it in your portfolio.

IT WORKS!
Learning Strategy:
Analyzing

The Sound of It: Understanding Intonation in Tag Questions

We often begin a conversation with a tag question. We add a "tag" to a sentence and it becomes a question. Our voice goes up if we aren't sure about the answer; it becomes a real question. Our voice goes down if we already know the answer and are making small talk.

EXAMPLES: We haven't met before, have we? (Voice goes up—the speaker isn't sure of the answer.)

We haven't met before, have we? (Voice goes down—the speaker knows the answer already.)

LEARNING STRATEGY

Forming Concepts: Making inferences (guesses) about a conversation helps you understand more than just the words.

A. Listen to the conversation. Where does it take place? Check the answer.

_____ **1.** in a supermarket

_____ **2.** in a school cafeteria

_____ **3.** in a health-food store

LEARNING STRATEGY

Remembering New Material: Repeating correct intonation helps you remember how to use it.

B. Listen and repeat.

Unsure of the Answer	Sure of the Answer
1. The food is awful, isn't it?	The food is awful, isn't it?
2. You don't see any fresh fruit, do you?	You don't see any fresh fruit, do you?
3. There isn't any yogurt is there?	There isn't any yogurt, is there?
4. There's lots of sugar, isn't there?	There's lots of sugar, isn't there?
5. You haven't seen a good health-food place, have you?	You haven't seen a good health-food place, have you?

Grammar Note: Contractions

COMMON CONTRACTIONS

I + am	=	I'm
you + are	=	you're
she + is	=	she's
he + is	=	he's
it + is	=	it's
we + are	=	we're
they + are	=	they're
are + not	=	aren't
is + not	=	isn't
should + not	=	shouldn't
do + not	=	don't
does + not	=	doesn't
has + not	=	hasn't
have + not	=	haven't
can + not	=	can't
will + not	=	won't

C. Listen to these sentences. Are the speakers unsure or sure of the answers? Put checkmarks on the lines.

REAL QUESTIONS (UNSURE OF THE ANSWER)	SMALL TALK (SURE OF THE ANSWER)
1. _____	_____
2. _____	_____
3. _____	_____
4. _____	_____
5. _____	_____
6. _____	_____
7. _____	_____
8. _____	_____

D. Work with a partner. Have a very short conversation for each situation. One person begins with a tag question (with the voice going *down* at the end). The other person answers. Use the cue words.

EXAMPLE:

SITUATION	**CUE WORDS**
Two people are at a bus stop.	A: bus / late again
	B: yes / wish it / be on time

Student A: The bus is late again, isn't it?

Student B: Yes, it is. I wish it would be on time.

SITUATIONS	CUE WORDS
1. Two people are in the produce section of a market.	A: tomatoes / not very ripe B: no / wish the stores / have *red* tomatoes
2. Two people are in line at a supermarket.	A: line / really long B: yes / wish they / open another register
3. Two people are at a party.	A: the music / loud B: yes / wish they / play a little softer
4. Two students are walking out of class.	A: class / really hard B: yes / wish the teacher / speak more slowly
5. Two neighbors are walking out of their apartment building.	A: it / really cold B: yes / wish spring / come a little faster
6. Two students are in line to register for classes.	A: line / not moving B: no / wish they / get some more clerks

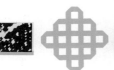

PART THREE: USEFUL EXPRESSIONS

Before You Listen

Work with a partner. Look at the pictures on page 35. What do you say in each situation? There are many possible answers.

Listening

You will hear four short conversations. Look at the pictures on this page. Which conversation goes with each picture? Listen and write the number (1, 2, 3, or 4) in the box next to the appropriate picture.

After You Listen

A. Work with a partner. Choose one of these situations. Write a short conversation. You might want to use some of the expressions in the boxes. Your teacher may ask you to put it on tape. Put it in your portfolio.

Situation 1: You are walking with a friend at school. You meet another friend. Introduce your two friends. Tell something about each one. Then tell the friend you met where the two of you are going. Have a short conversation. Then say good-bye.

Situation 2: Someone comes up to you at a party. You don't remember the person, but the person knows your name and says that the two of you met before. Say that you are sorry and ask where you met. Tell the person that it was nice to talk to him or her again.

Situation 3: Telephone a friend who gave you a present. Say something about what the present was and express thanks. Then say good-bye.

Situation 4: You and your boyfriend (girlfriend) had a fight. Telephone to say that you're sorry. Your boyfriend (girlfriend) is also sorry and thanks you for calling. You say good-bye.

Useful Expressions

INTRODUCING SOMEONE	RESPONSES
I'd like you to meet . . .	Nice (glad, pleased) to meet you.
This is . . . a friend of mine (my sister, etc.).	
Have you met . . . ?	

ENDING A CONVERSATION	
Good-bye.	
So long.	
See you (later, Friday, etc.).	
Have a good day. Have a good weekend.	
I have to go now, but I'll see (call) you . . .	
It's been good seeing you (talking to you).	
Talk to you soon.	
Keep in touch.	

EXPRESSING THANKS	RESPONSES
Thanks.	You're welcome.
Thank you very much (so much).	Don't mention it.
That was very kind of you.	
How thoughtful!	
I appreciate it. I'm very grateful.	

SAYING THAT YOU ARE SORRY	
I'm very sorry.	No problem.
Excuse me.	That's okay. That's all right.
Forgive me.	Don't worry about it.
It was my fault.	

B. Practice beginning a conversation, making small talk, and ending the conversation outside of class. You can do this any time. Complete this chart.

*IT WORKS!
Learning Strategy:
Looking for Practice
Opportunities*

DATE	PERSON I MADE SMALL TALK WITH	WHAT WE TALKED ABOUT	MY REACTION (FEELING) ABOUT THE CONVERSATION
____	_____	_____	_____
____	_____	_____	_____
____	_____	_____	_____
____	_____	_____	_____
____	_____	_____	_____
____	_____	_____	_____
____	_____	_____	_____
____	_____	_____	_____

SELF-EVALUATION

Here is a list of some things that you studied in this chapter. How did you do on each item? Check your answers.

	I UNDERSTAND THIS PRETTY WELL	I LEARNED SOMETHING, BUT I NEED TO LEARN MORE	I DON'T UNDERSTAND THIS
I studied:			
some good things to do to learn a language	____	____	____
how to begin a conversation	____	____	____
how to make small talk	____	____	____
how to understand intonation in tag questions (Is the speaker sure or unsure of the answer?)	____	____	____
how to introduce someone	____	____	____
how to say I'm sorry	____	____	____
how to express thanks	____	____	____
how to end a conversation	____	____	____

What's one thing that you would like to improve about your listening or speaking in the next chapter?

I'm going to work on ...

_____

_____

_____

Threads

English is the official language of 87 countries in the world.

Universal Almanac

This Is Who I Am

This chapter has three parts. You'll listen to people talking about their lives, and you'll tell others about your own life. Look at this list of some of the things that you'll study in the chapter. What's most important for you to learn? Put a 1. What's next most important? Put a 2, etc.

I WANT TO LEARN:

A. about other students' interests _____

B. to tell people about my life _____

C. how to understand meaning from intonation
(tone of voice) _____

D. how to ask people about their interests _____

E. to understand people when they speak fast _____

F. how to ask questions when I don't
understand someone _____

G. to get the main idea when I listen
(even if I don't understand every word) _____

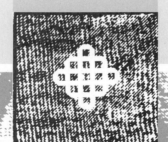

Look at the pictures and read the information. Why are these people famous? Do you know anything about their lives?

"My girlfriend and I were always coming up with things like making our dolls have beauty contests. We'd have pajama parties in someone's backyard tent, and I'd hold a flashlight to my face and tell some horror story. . . .

"I had my first date in my junior year and thought, well, as last it's finally starting. And then he never asked me out again. . . .

"One of the things I've found most appealing about adulthood is that you can be in charge of yourself and your fate. I like that."

Geena Davis, *People Magazine* (June 24, 1991).

Gérard Depardieu was the third of six in a family that he describes as "poorer than poor." He says, "It's good for an actor to be raised in poverty. The poor dream more."

Gérard Depardieu, *People Magazine* (February 4, 1991).

"I'm 63, and I've never had a house. . . . I started out like everyone else: a normal childhood, but then came a strange orphanhood—father and mother arrested and no one knowing whether they were alive or not. Later, after the war, we had a room in a communal apartment—there were 48 people in one apartment and one toilet."

Yelena Bonner, *Newsweek* (June 2, 1986).

QUESTIONS

1. Which person seemed to have a happy childhood?
2. Which person grew up without parents for some time?
3. What does Davis enjoy about being an adult?
4. Why does Depardieu believe that it's good for an actor to grow up poor?

Before You Listen

A. Read these questions and think about the answers.
1. In your culture, do high school or college students sometimes have a job? If so, what are typical jobs?
2. What was the first job you ever had? What kind of experience was it? (Was it good? Bad? Funny? Interesting?)
3. What kind of childhood did you have? (Was it happy? Difficult?) What are your most vivid (clearest) memories of your family?
4. Do friends sometimes come to visit you unexpectedly (without calling first)? If so, is your house always neat and clean, or is it sometimes messy?

LEARNING STRATEGY

Managing Your Learning: If you think about a subject before you listen to people talk about it, you understand more.

B. You're going to hear two people talk about their lives. One will talk about a memory of her first job. The other, Garrison Keillor,* will talk about a memory of his childhood. Before you listen, guess the meanings of the underlined words in the sentences below.
1. The <u>store detectives</u> caught the thief. He was trying to steal a jacket.
2. She's a <u>shoplifter</u>. She steals things from stores and puts them in her purse or coat.
3. He's a terrible <u>racist</u>. He doesn't like anyone who isn't white, like him.
4. I don't <u>trust</u> him. I don't believe his brother, either.
5. The child <u>burst into tears</u>. He couldn't stop crying.
6. He's such a <u>vain</u> person. He's always looking at himself in the mirror and worrying about his appearance.
7. We had a kind of "<u>low-medium level</u>" of housekeeping. In other words, the house wasn't always very clean.
8. They cleaned the house quickly because <u>company</u> was coming. They were happy to have guests, but they weren't really ready for them.

IT WORKS!

Learning Strategy: Guessing

* Reprinted by permission of Garrison Keillor. Copyright © 1991 by Garrison Keillor.

Listening

PERSON 1

LEARNING STRATEGY

Forming Concepts: Sometimes you need to listen for details (small points), not just main ideas.

IT WORKS!
Learning Strategy:
Making Inferences

A. Read these sentences. Then listen to Person 1. Why didn't she like her job in the department store? Check the answers. (There are several.)

_____ **1.** The job was boring.

_____ **2.** Her boss was a racist.

_____ **3.** Her salary was low.

_____ **4.** She spent all her money at the store.

_____ **5.** She wasn't good at her job.

B. The speaker didn't enjoy her job as a store detective. How do you think she feels about the experience now? Why do you think that? Discuss your answer with one other student.

PERSON 2

A. Look at the pictures below. What's happening in each?
B. As you listen to the speaker, put numbers in the small boxes (What happened first? Second? Third?, etc.)

Threads

When the guests have gone, the host is at peace.

Chinese proverb

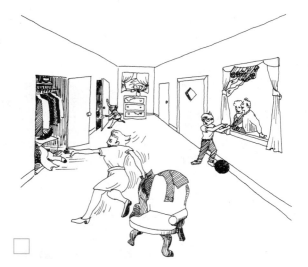

After You Listen

Managing Your Learning: Organizing your ideas before speaking gives you confidence.

NOW YOU CHOOSE

Think of one experience from your past. Organize your ideas about it and make notes. What happened? How did you feel about it? How do you feel about it now? Did you learn something from this experience? If you need some vocabulary words, look them up and write them down. Then tell this experience to a small group of students (three to four people). Choose *one* of these topics.

IT WORKS!
Learning Strategy:
Analyzing

1. an experience from your childhood
2. a memory of a family member (mother, grandfather, cousin, etc.)
3. something unusual that your family used to do
4. your first day of school *or* your first date *or* your first job
5. a memory of a teacher from elementary school
6. an experience that changed your life

Note: In your group, be sure to listen carefully when the other students speak. Express encouragement. When they finish, feel free to ask them questions.

43

| EXPRESSING ENCOURAGEMENT |

It's important to respond to someone who is telling you a story, just to let them know you're interested in what they are saying. Here are some expressions for this.

Right.	and?
Okay.	Well?
Yeah.	And then?
Yes?	And so?

The Sound of It: Listening for Stressed Words

In English, people stress (emphasize) the important words in a sentence. If you understand the stressed words, you can understand the important information.

How do you know which words are stressed? They are *higher* (the voice goes up), *louder,* and *clearer* than the other words. Listen for the "mountains" in speech—not the "valleys." The meaning of a sentence can change if the stress changes.

EXAMPLES: I liked Anna. (normal stress)
I <u>LIKED</u> Anna (but I don't like her now).
I liked <u>ANNA</u> (but I didn't like her brother).
<u>I</u> liked Anna (but other people didn't like her).

A. Listen to these sentences and repeat them. Notice the stressed words.
1. It was a TERRIBLE day.
2. WE'LL take those.
3. I was SUPPOSED to catch shoplifters.
4. They're going to TAKE something.
5. I couldn't SEE anything.
6. Go up and clean the BATHROOM.

B. Listen to the important (stressed) words in these sentences. Underline them.

1. This is my family.
2. I don't remember.
3. My brother saw it.
4. We had a test yesterday.
5. We had a test yesterday.
6. It was a horrible experience.
7. The job was kind of boring.
8. George used to work there.
9. George used to work there.

C. Work with a partner. Figure out (decide) which word needs to be stressed in each answer below. Underline it. When you finish all six, listen to the tape to see if you were right. Then practice saying the questions and answers.

1. Question: WHOSE father fixed breakfast?
   Answer: My father fixed breakfast.
2. Question: WHAT did your father FIX?
   Answer: My father fixed breakfast.
3. Question: What do you THINK?
   Answer: I think it's a good idea.
4. Question: What do YOU think?
   Answer: I think it's a good idea.
5. Question: Where did they GO?
   Answer: They went to the zoo.
6. Question: Where did THEY go?
   Answer: They went to the zoo.

D. With your partner, figure out which word needs to be stressed in each question and answer below. Underline it. Then listen to the tape to check your answers. Repeat each question and answer after the speaker.

1. Question: Where did you drive?
   Answer: I drove downtown.
2. Question: How did you get downtown?
   Answer: I drove downtown.
3. Question: Who drove downtown?
   Answer: I drove downtown.

IT WORKS!
Learning Strategy:
Brainstorming

PART TWO: THIS IS WHERE I AM

Before You Listen

A. What do people do for fun, in their free time? Write as many activities as you can think of on the lines below.

PHYSICAL ACTIVITIES	MENTAL ACTIVITIES	OTHER ACTIVITIES
skating (roller & ice)	*reading*	*sailing*

B. Share your ideas with a partner. Add any new activities to your list. Then share your ideas with the whole class. Add any new activities to your list.

Listening

You'll hear six people talk about their interests. They all answer the question. "What do you do in your free time?" Listen for the important words—the speakers' interests—and write them on the lines. Don't write other words. Use gerunds (words that end in *-ing*) or nouns. Listen two or three times.

Person 1: _____

Person 2: _____

Person 3: **a.** _____   **b.** _____   **c.** _____

Person 4: **a.** _____   **b.** _____

         c. _____   **d.** _____

Person 5: **a.** _____   **b.** _____   **c.** _____

         d. _____   **e.** _____

Person 6: **a.** _____   **b.** _____

         c. _____   **d.** _____

IT WORKS!
Learning Strategy →
Getting Information

After You Listen

GRAMMAR NOTE: GERUNDS AND INFINITIVES

After some verbs (such as enjoy), use a noun or a gerund (a word that ends in -ing).

EXAMPLES: I enjoy sports. (noun)

                    I enjoy exercising. (gerund)

After other verbs (such as like), use a noun, a gerund, or an infinitive (to + verb).

EXAMPLES: I like sports.

                    I like exercising

                    I like to exercise.

A. Talk with your classmates, teacher, people at your school, and people in your community. Ask them the question, "What do you do in your free time?" Complete the chart below with their answers. (Note: When a classmate asks *you* this question, answer with the verb *enjoy* or *like*.)

ASKING FOR CLARIFICATION

If you don't understand someone, it's important to ask a question. Here are some questions that you can ask:

Excuse me?

What was that again?

What is that?

How do you spell that?

PERSON'S NAME	INTERESTS/ACTIVITIES
_____	_____
_____	_____
_____	_____
_____	_____
_____	_____
_____	_____
_____	_____
_____	_____
_____	_____
_____	_____
_____	_____

B. In a small group, discuss your charts. Which activities seem to be most popular? Which are most relaxing? Which are most active? Which are most unusual?

_____

_____

_____

_____

The Sound of It: Understanding Intonation in Questions with *Or*

There are two kinds of questions with the word *or*: *yes/no* questions and *either/or* questions.

1. In *yes/no* questions, the answer is "Yes" or "No." The speaker's voice goes up two times.
   EXAMPLE: Question: Would you like coffee or tea?
   Answer: Yes, please.

2. In *either/or* questions, the answer is one of the two items from the question. The speaker's voice goes up on the first item and down on the second item.
   EXAMPLE: Question: Would you like coffee or tea?
   Answer: Tea, please.

A. Listen to these questions and repeat them. Notice the intonation.

YES/NO QUESTIONS	*EITHER/OR* QUESTIONS
1. Do you like TV or movies?	Do you like TV or movies?
2. Does she enjoy ice skating or roller skating?	Does she enjoy ice skating or roller skating?
3. Does he swim at the gym or at home?	Does he swim at the gym or at home?
4. Is he an actor or a musician?	Is he an actor or a musician?
5. Did she work during the summer or after school?	Did she work during the summer or after school?

B. Listen to the intonation in each question. Is it a *yes/no* question or an *either/or* question? For each *yes/no* question, write *yes* on the line. For each *either/or* question, write one of the two items from the question.

1. _____   6. _____

2. _____   7. _____

3. _____   8. _____

4. _____   9. _____

5. _____   10. _____

C. Which of the questions below are *yes/no* questions? Which are *either/or* questions? Work with a partner and decide on the intonation for each question. Then practice saying it.
   1. Question: Do they enjoy water skiing or snow skiing?
      Answer: Snow skiing.
   2. Question: Do you like classical music or jazz?
      Answer: Jazz.
   3. Question: Does she travel on weekends or during the summer?
      Answer: Yes.

4. Question: Does he spend much time with his friends or family?
Answer: No.

5. Question: Do they eat at good restaurants or fast-food places?
Answer: Usually at fast-food places.

D. Take turns with your partner asking and answering these questions. When you *ask,* choose which intonation you want: *yes/no* or *either/or.* When you *answer,* be sure to listen carefully to your partner's intonation so that you can use correct intonation in the answer.

1. Do they go dancing on Fridays or Saturdays?
2. Does he like swimming or surfing?
3. Do you live with your family or a friend?
4. Does she do her homework during the week or on weekends?
5. Do you like Chinese food or Italian food?
6. Do you enjoy walking or jogging?

PART THREE: THIS IS WHERE I'M GOING

Before You Listen

A. Read this selection by Yelena Bonner, widow of Andrei Sakharov. She wrote this in 1986, before her husband died. Then answer the questions.

A QUIRKY FAREWELL TO AMERICA

"Americans do not want war. What Americans want is a house. The house is a symbol of independence.

"I also want a house in addition to my usual wants that everyone be together and healthy and that there be no war. With enough land around it, and no more, for me to plant flowers. . . . I don't need a lot of bedrooms, just one for us and one for Mother, a guest room, and one more so that I'm always ready for our grandchildren.

"My dream, my own house, is unattainable for my husband and myself, as unattainable as heaven on earth. But I want a house. If not for me, then for my son and his family in America."

Yelena Bonner, "A Quirky Farewell to America," *Newsweek* (June 2, 1986), p. 45.

1. What is Bonner's dream?
2. In her opinion, why is a house important to Americans?
3. Does she think that her dream can come true? In other words, is her dream attainable?

B. You're going to hear four people talk about their goals and dreams. People's goals usually change as they get older. In groups, discuss these questions.

1. What are some possible goals and dreams of teenagers in high school?

2. When young adults (in their twenties and thirties) think about the future, what might be some of their goals and dreams?

3. What are some possible goals and dreams of middle-aged people (in their forties and fifties)?

4. When older people (in their sixties and seventies) think about the future, what might some of their goals and dreams be?

Listening

A. Listen to the four speakers. They don't tell their ages. Try to guess how old they are. Write the numbers (1, 2, 3, or 4) in the blanks.

Person _____ is probably a teenager.

Person _____ is probably a young adult.

Person _____ is probably middle-aged.

Person _____ is probably older.

LEARNING STRATEGY

Forming Concepts: Taking notes can help you understand and remember what a speaker says.

B. The speakers talked about their goals. They also discussed their plans to reach these goals. Listen again, as many times as you need to. What are their goals, and how do they plan to reach them? Take notes. Do not write complete sentences. The first one is an example.

PERSON 1

Goal:

to give my daughter a good life

Plans to reach this goal:

buy a house with a garden, change work times,

save money for her college education.

PERSON 2

Goal:

_____

_____

_____

Plans to reach this goal:

_____

_____

_____

PERSON 3

Goal:

_____

_____

_____

Plans to reach this goal:

_____

_____

_____

PERSON 4

Goal:

_____

_____

_____

Plans to reach this goal:

_____

_____

_____

Threads

In 1990, 6.2 millon American teenagers had a full- or part-time job.

U.S. Department of Labor,
Bureau of Statistics

After You Listen

GRAMMAR NOTE: *BE GOING TO* AND *WILL*

When you talk about future plans, use be going to + verb.

EXAMPLES: I'm going to go to college.

He's going to become a lawyer.

When you talk about future predictions, use be going to + verb or will + verb.

EXAMPLES: She's going to work with animals.

They'll live here for a few years.

I won't retire for another twenty years.

A. Now You Choose. Think of your goals and dreams for the future. These can be goals for yourself, your family and friends, your community, or the world. Choose two of these topics:
1. education
2. relationships with other people
3. work/profession
4. money
5. place to live
6. peace; the environment
7. other: _____
On the lines below, write your goals and your plans to reach these goals. Just write notes; don't write sentences. (Use page 51 as an example.) Then put this page in your portfolio.

Goal/dream:

_____

Plans to reach this goal:

_____

_____

Goal/dream:

_____

Plans to reach this goal:

_____

_____

B. Tell another student about your goals and plans.

The Sound of It: Understanding Reductions

A. In normal or fast speech, you will hear "reductions" of some words. Listen to these examples. Can you hear the difference between the long forms and the short forms?

LONG FORM	REDUCTION	SHORT FORM
What do you do?	what do you → whadaya*	Whadaya* do?
What are you doing?	what are you → whatcha*	Whatcha* doing?
What kind of childhood was it?	kind of → kinda*	What kinda* childhood was it?
What did you do?	did you → didja*	What didja* do?
What did he do?	did he → didee*	What didee* do?
They used to live here.	used to → yoosta*	They yoosta* live here.
I'm going to buy a house.	going to → gonna*	I'm gonna* buy a house.

*These forms are not correct in writing.

B. Listen to these sentences. Do you hear a reduction? Check *Long Form* or *Short Form* as you listen.

	LONG FORM	SHORT FORM
Examples:		
a. <u>What are you</u> looking at?	_____	X
b. <u>What are you</u> looking at?	X	_____
I. <u>Did you</u> enjoy school?	_____	_____
2. I'm <u>going to</u> study history.	_____	_____
3. What <u>kind of</u> sports do you like?	_____	_____
4. He <u>used to</u> live with his grandmother.	_____	_____
5. Where <u>did he</u> go to school?	_____	_____
6. <u>What do you</u> think about it?	_____	_____
7. I'm <u>kind of</u> tired.	_____	_____
8. How are you <u>going to</u> do it?	_____	_____
9. Why <u>did you</u> do that?	_____	_____
10. <u>What do you</u> want to do?	_____	_____

C. Listen to these conversations. You'll hear reduced (short) forms. Write the long forms.

1. A: _____ see that movie on TV last night?

B: Yeah. I thought it was _____ be funny, but it was really sad.

2. A: What _____ sports do you like?

B: Oh, tennis, swimming, basketball. I _____ play tennis in high school.

3. A: _____ planning to do on the weekend?

B: Bob and I are _____ look for a new car.

_____ tell you about the accident with the old car?
A: Yeah. That's too bad.

SELF-EVALUATION

Here is a list of some things that you studied in this chapter. How did you do on each item? Check your answers.

	I DID WELL	I DID OKAY, BUT I NEED MORE PRACTICE	I DIDN'T DO WELL
I studied:			
telling people about my life	____	____	____
asking people about their interests	____	____	____
understanding meaning from intonation	____	____	____
understanding people when they speak fast	____	____	____
asking questions when I didn't understand	____	____	____
getting the main idea	____	____	____

What's one thing that you would like to improve about your listening or speaking in the next chapter?

I'm going to work on . . .

_____

_____

Threads

My interest is in the future because I am going to spend the rest of my life there.

Charles F. Kettering

Health: Getting the Most out of Life

*T*his chapter has six parts. You'll find out some things about how to feel your best and some practical things about ordering food in English. Look at this list of some of the things that you'll study in this chapter. What's most important for your to learn? Put a 1. What's next most important? Put a 2, etc.

I WANT TO LEARN:

A. **how to understand menus and order food in restaurants** _____
B. **about restaurant customs** _____
C. **how to understand charts and interviews about healthful foods, exercise, and stress** _____
D. **how to give advice about health** _____
E. **how to hear the difference between *can* and *can't*** _____
F. **about people's habits and life styles 10,000 years ago** _____
G. **about some older people's advice on how to stay young** _____

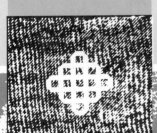

Look at the pictures and read the information.

IT WORKS!
Learning Strategy:
Discussing Your
Feelings

"The single most important thing to know about Americans . . . is that Americans think that death is optional (a choice). . . . Your life is in your own hands . . . and the quality of that life also. You owe it to yourself to be beautiful, clever, thin, successful, and healthy. If you fail, it's because you're not trying hard enough . . . (you didn't run regularly, you should've eaten more bran). Death becomes your fault."

Adapted from Jane Walmsley, *Brit-think/Ameri-think: A Transatlantic Survival Guide* (New York: Penguin Books, 1987).

There are times when it's good to get mad and let the world know it. But there's also the possibility of taking the energy of anger and putting it to work for positive purposes . . . Many studies suggest that people with a positive attitude about life suffer less sickness.

George Leonard, "Tap Your Hidden Energy," *Reader's Digest* (September, 1988).

Dr. William Fry, Jr., a Stanford University researcher, has studied the beneficial (good) effects of laughter for more than thirty years. "When we laugh," Fry explains, "muscles are activated. When we stop laughing, these muscles relax. Many people with arthritis, rheumatism, and other painful conditions benefit greatly from a healthy dose of laughter. Many headache sufferers feel the same relief."

Nancy and Dean Hoch, "Take Time to Laugh," *Reader's Digest* (February, 1988).

DISCUSSION

1. Do you "take time to laugh"? When do you laugh most?
2. What kinds of things make you angry? Give an example of a time when you felt angry.

Before You Listen

IT WORKS!
Learning Strategy:
Identifying

A. Work with a partner. Look at the chart about foods that heal (make you well) and foods that kill. Match the names of the foods to the pictures. Draw lines. Figs and dates are dried fruits; there are no pictures of these two foods.

B. Read the notes under the pictures and answer these questions.

1. Which foods are high in *fiber*?

2. What do you think *fiber* means?

_____ **a.** fat

_____ **b.** salt

_____ **c.** substance (in a plant, cells that give strength and support)

3. What diseases do foods with fiber help prevent?

4. What do "Omega-3 fatty acids" help prevent? What foods have these acids?

5. *Calories* are units of heat, or energy. Which fish has more calories per serving:

_____ **a.** cod

_____ **b.** sole or flounder

_____ **c.** canned tuna

6. What do you think *excessive* alcohol means?

_____ **a.** too much

_____ **b.** too little

7. What do prime rib, fried chicken, biscuits and gravy (meat sauce with milk or water and flour), fried eggs, and cheese have in common:

_____ **a.** They have a lot of sugar.

_____ **b.** They are very good for you.

_____ **c.** They have a lot of fat.

10 Vegetable Foods That Heal

FOOD	Grams of Fiber*
Bran Cereals	2-14
Medium Sweet Potato	10
1/2 Cup of Baked Beans With Tomato Sauce	9
1/2 Cup of Dried Figs	9
1/2 Cup of Dried Dates	8
1 Cup of Broccoli	7
1 Cup of Brussels Sprouts	7
1 Ear, Corn on the Cob	7
1/2 Cup Kidney Beans	7
1/2 Cup Lima Beans	7

*High fiber foods like these have been proven to help prevent colon cancer and reverse heart disease.

Three Meats That Heal

FOOD	Calories Per Serving	Grams of Fat	% Calories From Fat
Cod	89	.7	7%
Sole/Flounder	99	1.3	12%
Canned Tuna in Water	116	2.1	16%

High in Omega-3 fatty acids, proven to reverse heart disease

...And 6 Foods That Kill

The following foods are proven to increase your risk of heart disease, stroke, high blood pressure, colon cancer and other diseases:

- PRIME RIB ■ FRIED CHICKEN
- BISCUITS & GRAVY
- FRIED EGG ■ CHEESE
- EXCESSIVE ALCOHOL

Listening

A. You will hear two conversations that take place in a restaurant. In Conversation 1 a woman is ordering a meal, and in Conversation 2 a man is ordering a meal. Listen to both conversations and answer this question:

Who cares more about health, the man or the woman?

B. Read the following list of foods and drinks. Then listen to the conversations again. Write *M* next to the foods or drinks that the man orders. Write *W* next to the foods or drinks that the woman orders. You may have to listen several times.

MAIN DISHES

_____ prime rib

_____ steak

_____ pork chops

_____ fried chicken

_____ sole

_____ cod

SIDE DISHES

_____ rice

_____ potatoes (mashed, baked, or french fried)

_____ corn on the cob

_____ sweet potatoes

_____ baked beans

_____ biscuits and gravy

_____ (green) salad

_____ vegetable beef soup

DESSERTS

_____ lemon cake

_____ strawberries

_____ apple pie

_____ ice cream

_____ fruit salad

_____ chocolate pie

BEVERAGES

_____ coffee

_____ tea

_____ milk

_____ orange juice

After You Listen

A. Work with a partner. Look at the menu from Lyon's Restaurant on page 61 or at a menu from a local restaurant that your teacher brings to class. One person is the waiter or waitress and one person is the customer. Have a conversation. Your teacher may ask you to present it to the class or put it on tape for your portfolio. Don't forget to include:
   1. finding out and telling about the "specials" (what they are and how much they cost)
   2. asking and answering questions about foods on the menu
   3. getting the check

Ordering Food in a Restaurant

WAITER:	CUSTOMER:
May I take your order?	What do you recommend?
What would you like?	What's the special today?
Would you like . . . with that?	How much is that?
How is everything here?	What's the soup of the day?
May I take your plate?	I'll have . . . / I'd like . . .
Would you like coffee or dessert?	May I have the check, please?

Salads

Fresh Fruit Salad 6.95
A combination of luscious seasonal fresh fruit, served on a bed of mixed greens. Your choice of cottage cheese, frozen yogurt or sherbet.

SPECIAL SALADS
Fresh and delicious with mixed greens, seasonal vegetables and your choice of dressings: Ranch, Non-fat Italian, Bleu Cheese or 1000 Island. Roll and butter included.
NEW! **Try Our Honey Mustard Dressing.**

NEW! **Oriental Chicken Salad** 6.95
Strips of chicken breast atop a mixture of salad greens, tossed with honey ginger sesame dressing, almonds and mandarin oranges.

Cobb Salad 6.95
Breast of turkey, crumbled bleu cheese, bacon, tomato, egg and avocado, on a bed of mixed greens with your choice of dressing.

Shrimp Louie 7.25
A generous portion of succulent bay shrimp.

Chicken Fajita Salad 6.95
Breast of chicken pieces, lightly spiced and grilled with mushrooms, onions, and red and green bell peppers. Served warm.

Tuna Neptune 6.25
Dolphin-safe, all white albacore tuna salad.

Desserts

PIES ... Fresh Daily

Hot Apple Pie with Cinnamon Sauce ... 1.95
A la mode add .75

Chocolate Cream Pie 2.25
Our own special recipe. Rich chocolate whipped with thick, sweet cream and piled high in a tender, flaky crust. Topped with real whipped cream and chocolate sprinkles.

Specialty Pies
Ask your server for today's featured pies.

TAKE THE CAKE

Heavenly Chocolate Cake 2.15
Four-layer double chocolate cake made with a mixture of Dutch and semi-sweet chocolate with a rich fudge icing.

Three-Layer Carrot Cake. 2.15
Our moist, luscious carrot cake with rich cream cheese frosting.

Cheesecake Supreme. 2.35
Topped with hot fudge, blueberry or strawberry topping and chopped nuts.

Creamy Cheesecake. 2.15
Dairy fresh, rich and velvety on a graham cracker crust.

Entrées

POPULAR COMBOS

Steak and Shrimp ... 9.55
USDA choice top sirloin steak with a Lyon's share of golden fried shrimp.

Steak and Chicken 9.25
Grilled breast of chicken served teriyaki or lemon style with a broiled top sirloin steak.

Chicken and Shrimp 8.95
Grilled breast of chicken served teriyaki or lemon style with lots of golden fried shrimp.

BEEF

New York Steak 10.25
Broiled USDA choice 10 oz. New York.

Teriyaki Steak 9.45
Grilled USDA choice 8 oz. sirloin steak.

Liver 'n Onions 7.85
With bacon, add 85 cents.

Prime Rib Special
It's prime time daily!! From 4 p.m.-10 p.m. Try our thick, juicy cut of tender prime rib, served au jus with horseradish sauce.
New Lower Price!. . . 8.95

Extra Thick Cut: add $1.50

LYON'S SPECIALTIES

Baby Back Ribs 9.95
A full rack of meaty, tender pork ribs in zesty barbecue sauce.

Lyon's Chicken 7.95
Grilled boneless breast of chicken served teriyaki, lemon or barbecue style.

NEW! **Southern Fried Chicken** 7.95
Four pieces of tender, golden fried chicken with mashed potatoes and country gravy.

CHICKEN AND SEAFOOD

Chicken Cashew Stir Fry* 7.95
In teriyaki sauce with fresh mushrooms and Chinese vegetables. Served on rice.

Chicken Pasta Supreme* 7.85
Grilled chicken, mushrooms and fresh vegetables in Alfredo sauce on fettucine. With garlic bread.

English Style Fish and Chips 7.95
Hand-dipped in beer batter and deep fried.

Shrimps Galore 8.95
A platter of golden fried breaded shrimp.

FRESH FISH
We offer two or more fresh fish daily. Ask your server about today's fresh catches. Served grilled, or most fish can be broiled, if you prefer.

Priced daily ... from 7.95 to 9.65

* Potato/rice and/or vegetables not included.

B. Write the conversation from your role-play and put it in your portfolio.

C. Go to a restaurant where people speak English and then answer these questions.

   1. How did people get the waiter's attention? (How do you get the waiter's attention in your culture?)

   2. What specials did the restaurant have? How much did they cost?

   3. Sometimes you pay at the table—the waiter or waitress takes your money—and sometimes at the cash register. (Often the check says, "Please pay at the register.") How did you get the check? How did you pay? Did you leave a tip?

IT WORKS!
Learning Strategy:
Looking for Practice
Opportunities

Before You Listen

A. Exercise is one way to increase your energy level. Exercise helps the brain produce natural tranquilizers and so it also fights stress, or tension. Read the following chart, a guide to weekly exercise.

Column A	Column B	Column C	Column D	Column E
Aerobic exercise	Everyday activities	Strength training	Fun and games	Flexibility and stress reduction
walk 20 minutes	garden 20 minutes	free weights 20 minutes	row 30 minutes	yoga class or 30-minute at-home session
swim 12 minutes	play an instrument 25 minutes	gymnastics 30 minutes	play baseball 1 hour	stretching class or 30 minute at-home session
run 1 mile	scrub a floor 16 minutes	calisthenics (pushups, situps) 20 minutes	play tennis 1 hour	T'ai chi ch'uan class or 30 minute at-home session
ride a bike (outside) 3 miles	chop wood 16 minutes	body-sculpting class	box 30 minutes	self-defense class
aerobic dance 15 minutes	sweep 30 minutes		bowl 1 hour	
ride exercise bike 15 minutes	vacuum 40 minutes		dance (hip-hop) 30 minutes	
jump rope 10 minutes	paint house 22 minutes		dance (ballroom) 1 hour	
stair-climb (machine) 15 minutes	rake leaves 32 minutes		ski (downhill) 30 minutes	
	mow lawn (hand mower) 15 minutes		ski (cross-country) 30 minutes	
	shovel snow 15 minutes		horseback ride 1 hour	
			roller- or ice-skate 30 minutes	
			hike 30 minutes	
			sail 1 hour	
			do karate 30 minutes	
			play golf 40 minutes (no cart)	
			play soccer 30 minutes	

Daily fitness allowances (two per day)

Workout	A	B	C	D	E	Total calories burned
	☐	☐	☐	☐	☐	_____

"The Fitness Plan." Each week, do three to four exercises from Column A, two from Column C, and two from Column E. The activities in Columns A, B, C, and E burn (use) 100 calories each; the activities in D burn 200 calories each. Try to burn 1400 calories a week. You can do different kinds of activities to make your exercise plan more fun. You can use a box like the one above to record your exercise workouts each day. Your teacher will act out some of the activities from the chart. Look at the chart and tell what activity he or she is doing.

© Self, April 1992, pp. 145–146.

B. Work with a partner and answer these questions.
   1. How long do you have to work in the garden to burn 100 calories? How long do you have to play a musical instrument to burn 100 calories? Sweep the floor? Rake leaves?
   2. If you ride an exercise bike (a machine) indoors for fifteen minutes, you burn 100 calories. How far do you have to ride a bicycle outdoors to burn 100 calories? How long do you have to walk in order to burn 100 calories? Swim? Jump rope?
   3. Which burns more calories: rowing a boat for thirty minutes or vacuuming the floor for forty minutes?

IT WORKS!
Learning Strategy:
Understanding a
Chart

Listening

A. You will hear five people answer the question, "What do you do to get exercise?" On the chart on page 62 ("The Fitness Plan"), check the activities you hear. One of the activities is not on the chart.
B. Listen again. Did you hear an activity that is not on the chart? What is it?

IT WORKS!
Learning Strategy:
Getting Information

After You Listen

Ask four people the question, "What do you do to get exercise?" Write their answers below.

EXERCISE ACTIVITIES

Person 1: _____

Person 2: _____

Person 3: _____

Person 4: _____

LEARNING STRATEGY

Understanding and Using Emotion: Laughter relaxes you and increases your openness to the new language.

By permission of Johnny Hart and Creators Syndicate, Inc.

PART THREE: STRESS AND YOUR HEALTH

Before You Listen

. IT WORKS!
Learning Strategy:
Brainstorming

Work in groups and answer this question: In what situations do people feel tension, or stress? Make a short list with ideas from everyone in your group.

EXAMPLES: in traffic, at the dentist's office

_____

_____

_____

_____

_____

Listening

IT WORKS!
Learning Strategy:
Taking Notes

You are going to hear four people answer the question, "How does stress affect your health habits?" Write the answers, but do not write everything that they say. Write a short answer only. The first one is an example.

Person 1: ___*can't sleep*_____

Person 2: _____

Person 3: _____

Person 4: _____

After You Listen

IT WORKS!
Learning Strategy:
Working with Others

A. Work in groups. How does stress affect your health habits? Most people have a change in health habits when they feel stress; this is normal. Do you do any of the following things when you feel stress?
1. Eat more food? What type of food?
2. Eat less food?
3. Drink more alcohol?
4. Smoke more cigarettes?
5. Sleep more?
6. Sleep less? Wake up during the night?

In groups, make at least five sentences about how stress affects your health.

GRAMMAR NOTE: COMPARISON OF AMOUNTS

as much as	Do you eat as much (meat, food) as I do?
as many as	Can you eat as many (hamburgers, crackers) as I can?
more	He eats more (sweets, fruit) than his sister does.
less	He eats less (fruit, food) than she does.
fewer	I eat fewer eggs than I used to.
	Use *less* and *as much as* for noncount nouns (butter, cereal, etc.).
	Use *fewer* and *as many as* for count nouns (apples, oranges, etc.).

EXAMPLES: Monica eats more fast food, like hamburgers, and drinks more soft drinks, like Coca-Cola.
Midori eats less.
Tak sleeps fewer hours.
Jesús drinks more coffee.

B. Work in groups. Look at this list of how to eat right when you feel stress or tension. Have a conversation. One person tells about a situation that causes stress in his or her life (it doesn't have to be real). The other people give advice. Use *should, shouldn't,* or *ought to.* Note: *wanes* = decreases; *avoid* = stay away from.

Threads

Alcohol slows the body's abiltiy to burn fat. That's why many beer drinkers develop a large stomach.

VitaList

How to Eat Right When You're Stressed

■ Drink plenty of water.
■ Eat high-fiber foods.
■ Don't skip meals.
■ Focus on variety.
■ If you're ill, think nutrition.

■ If you're overeating, pay attention.
■ Eat less if your appetite wanes.
■ Avoid alcohol.
■ Cut back on caffeine.
■ Avoid sugary snacks.

© *Vitality Digest, November 1991, p. 21.*

EXAMPLE: My boyfriend (girlfriend) wants to get married. I'm not ready for that. So we've been fighting a lot.
You should . . .
You ought to . . .

GIVING ADVICE

You should (shouldn't) . . .
You ought (not) to . . .
You had better (not) . . .
I advise you (not) to . . .
I recommend that you (not) . . .

IT WORKS!
Learning Strategy:
Analyzing

The Sound of It: Listening for Stressed Words— *Can* or *Can't*?

In the interviews about stress and health habits, you hear several examples of *can* and *can't.* Listen to the examples again:

PERSON 1: I lie awake at night . . . can't go to sleep, thinking or worrying. Then I'm tired the next day and I can't think clearly.

PERSON 2: I can eat and eat and eat . . . anything.

PERSON 3: I start smoking more—one cigarette after another. Just can't stop.

PERSON 4: I can't eat.

Here are some more examples. Listen to the difference in stress.

I can RIDE a BIKE.
I CAN'T RIDE a BIKE.

He can RIDE a HORSE.
He CAN'T RIDE a HORSE.

Do you hear the difference? *Can't* is louder and clearer. Listen to these sentences. Do you hear *can* or *can't*? Check the answer.

	CAN	CAN'T
1.	✓____	____
2.	____	____
3.	____	____
4.	____	____
5.	____	____
6.	____	____
7.	____	____
8.	____	____
9.	____	____
10.	____	____

Threads

Children who live with smokers are more than twice as likely to develop lung cancer later in life than children of non-smoking parents.

Before You Listen

You are going to hear selections from an interview with a health expert. Before you listen, guess the meanings of the underlined words in the sentences below.

1. My <u>physician</u>, Dr. Jones, tells me that too much stress can hurt my health.
2. He advises me to eat foods with good things in them—vitamins, minerals, and other <u>nutrients</u>.
3. He says it's not possible to <u>utilize</u> all your energy, but you can use more of your hidden energy if you follow some simple steps.
4. Long ago Americans used to watch a funny TV show, "<u>Candid Camera</u>," with Allen Funt.
5. My grandmother helped my mother a lot for many years. My mother always asked me to thank my grandmother politely for things, to express our <u>gratitude</u>. She was very thankful that my grandmother gave her so much help.

IT WORKS!
Learning Strategy:
Guessing

Listening

A. You are going to hear two short selections from an interview with Dr. Joseph Houlton, a health expert.* Earlier in the interview, Dr. Houlton explained that sometimes stress is good for us. We need some stress in our lives in order to do certain kinds of activities (like talking to a group of people or playing music in a formal situation). He said that a fisherman might work in his garden to relax. A gardener might go fishing to relax. He then talked about stress and negative emotions, which can cause us to get sick. There are some difficult words in the interview, and you won't understand every word. Listen for main ideas only.

IT WORKS!
Learning Strategy:
Getting the Main Idea

Section 1: Listen to Section 1 and answer this question: Dr. Norman Cousins had a serious illness; the odds (chances) were against his recovery, and he thought he might die. What did he do to get well?

Section 2: Listen to Section 2 of the interview and answer this question: Dr. Houlton has a motto, or saying, on his business card. It tells the attitude he tries to have toward life. What is the saying? How does it help him in life?

* From the series "The Human Condition," KUT-FM; interviewed by Bert K. Smith of the Hogg Foundation for Mental Health, University of Texas, Austin, Texas 78712.

After You Listen

Write a motto, or saying, for yourself. It should tell how you can be happy in life. It can be something simple, like "Eat chocolate," or something like "Do something nice for someone every day." Put it in your portfolio.

PART FIVE: HOW PEOPLE LIVED 10,000 YEARS AGO

Before You Listen

There is a lot of talk today about "going back to nature"—eating natural foods, living a natural life style. But just how did people live thousands of years ago? You will hear a selection from a talk by Robert Pritikin of the Pritikin Institute. Before you listen, guess the meanings of the underlined words in the sentences below.

1. Early people were <u>hunter/gatherers</u>. They hunted animals to eat, and they also gathered plants.
2. Early people gathered roots or <u>tubers</u>. Examples of tubers we eat today are carrots and potatoes.
3. People would <u>dig</u> in the ground and find these roots or tubers to eat.
4. <u>Civilization</u> brought many changes: people began to live in larger groups and develop culture.
5. <u>Carbohydrates</u> are sugars and starches; carbohydrates are high in calories.

Listening

Robert Pritikin begins his talk like this: "I want you to imagine a world in which you are young and vital every day of your life. And in this world you can eat whenever you're hungry and you can eat 'til you're full, yet you're thin, you're lean, all through your life. You never even have to see a doctor unless you break a leg or get an infectious disease, or have a child. . . . Anybody here want to live in this fantasy world? . . . The catch is that you have to match your behavior to your biology."*

Listen to the next section of his talk. Which of these sentences are true, according to the speaker? Write *T* in the blank. Which are false?

* Source: Speech to the Common-wealth Club of California, January 31, 1992.

Write *F* in the blank. You will probably have to listen several times. Don't worry if you don't understand every word. Just listen for the information you need.

_____ **1.** People's diet 10,000 years ago was similar to our modern diet.

_____ **2.** People 10,000 years ago ate three meals a day.

_____ **3.** They were hunters who ate a lot of meat.

_____ **4.** They ate a lot of fiber.

_____ **5.** They got a lot of exercise.

After You Listen

A. For several days, make a list of foods that you eat. Write what you have for breakfast, lunch, dinner, and snacks. Then look at the "Food Guide Pyramid" on page 70. This shows how much of each type of food you should eat each day. Are you eating right? If not, what foods should you eat more of? Less of? (Remember that most fast foods—hamburgers, fried chicken, french fries, soft drinks—contain a lot of fat and sugar and are at the top of the pyramid.)

DAY 1

Breakfast _____

Lunch _____

Dinner _____

Snacks _____

DAY 2

Breakfast _____

Lunch _____

Dinner _____

Snacks _____

DAY 3

Breakfast _____

Lunch _____

Dinner _____

Snacks _____

Food Guide Pyramid
A guide to daily food choices

Fats, oils and sweets
Use sparingly

Milk, yogurt and
cheese
2-3 servings

Vegetable
groups
**3-5
servings**

Meat, poultry, fish,
dry beans, eggs
and nut groups
2-3 servings

Fruit groups
2-4 servings

Bread, cereal, rice and pasta groups
6-11 servings

United States Department of Agriculture

B. In American culture, there are certain sayings about foods from long ago. Fish is "brain food"; people say it's good for the brain. They say carrots are good for the eyes. Another saying is, "An apple a day keeps the doctor away" (meaning that you will be healthy if you eat an apple every day). In your culture, are there certain foods that people say are good for you? Ask four or five people this question and complete the chart.

	CULTURE/ COUNTRY	FOOD	SAYING
PERSON 1	_____	_____	_____ _____
PERSON 2	_____	_____	_____ _____
PERSON 3	_____	_____	_____ _____
PERSON 4	_____	_____	_____ _____
PERSON 5	_____	_____	_____ _____

C. Read the following paragraph and answer the questions.

Robert Pritikin says later in his talk that our teeth are perfect for eating vegetables—more like a horse's teeth than a tiger's teeth. Our mouth can move from side to side, like a horse's mouth, while a tiger's mouth moves up and down. And, like animals that eat only vegetables, we have livers that continue to produce cholesterol even if we eat cholesterol (things like egg yolks and butter). This means we get heart disease. He also says that we had to be able to get fat in order to survive, to have enough food for the winter in the form of fat. But these days "we are in an endless fall fattening up for a winter that never comes."

1. Do you think Robert Pritikin advises people to eat a lot of meat? Why or why not?
2. Do you think people go to his talks to find out how to gain weight or lose weight? Why?

CULTURAL NOTE

Did you know that . . .
—Before the invention of the refrigerator, Americans ate 1/4 as much fat as they do now?
—Before the invention of the light bulb, Americans slept 9 1/2 hours a night (about two hours a night more than they do now)?
—Smoking, drinking alcohol, and breathing other people's cigarette smoke are the three main causes of preventable deaths in the United States? That is, they are the three causes that people could avoid by changing their health habits.

PART SIX: IT'S A MATTER OF ATTITUDE

Before You Listen

Work in groups. You are going to hear part of a television show about older people.* Barbara de Angelis talks to some older Americans about their views of life. In groups, discuss these questions:

1. Do you know any very old people?
2. Are they happy? Are they active?
3. Do they give advice to younger people? If so, what do they say?

IT WORKS!
Learning Strategy:
Thinking Ahead about
a Subject

Listening

Listen to the selection from the television show and answer the questions. You may have to listen several times. You may not understand everything. Just listen for the answers to the questions. First, read the information and the questions on page 72.

*© 1991 100% Productions, Inc. Kushner-Locke Company. Used by permission

PERSON 1: LOTTIE HICKS, 105 YEARS OLD

Lottie Hicks celebrated her 102nd birthday by riding in a Goodyear Blimp (a kind of balloon) out to Catalina Island, near Los Angeles. She celebrated her 104th birthday by riding in a helicopter around Burbank and Hollywood. What does she want to do for her 106th birthday?

PERSON 2: MARY ANN WEBBER, 72 YEARS OLD

Mary Ann Webber says that when she was young she was afraid of making a fool of herself, but now she doesn't mind if people call her a "character" (a unique person). What does Mrs. Webber mean when she says that aging is "a matter of attitude"?

PERSON 3: LEO SALAZAR, 75 YEARS OLD

Leo Salazar lifts, or presses, weights—he can lift 75 pounds (his age) in weights. What else does he do?

After You Listen

Work in groups. Discuss these questions.

1. Are Lottie Hicks, Mary Ann Webber, and Leo Salazar like older people that you know?
2. Do you want to live to be 100 years old? Why or why not?

JUST FOR FUN

Ann Landers has a column in many newspapers across the United States every day. Here is one of her columns. It includes a "stress diet." Read it and answer this question: Would you like to go on a diet like this? Why or why not?

ANN LANDERS

A diet to die for

Dear Ann:
  During these tension-filled days, we are hearing a lot about stress. People need a good laugh.
  I am sending on a stress diet that a friend dropped in my mailbox last week. It really lifted my spirits. Please share it with your readers.
      —Kitty L.
        principal, S.S.E. School, Decatur, Ill.

The Stresser's Diet

Breakfast
1/2 grapefruit
1 piece whole-wheat toast
8 oz. skim milk

Lunch
4 oz. lean broiled chicken
1 cup steamed lima beans
1 Oreo cookie
Herb tea

Midafternoon snack
Rest of the package of Oreo cookies
Quart of rocky-road ice cream
Jar of hot-fudge sauce

Dinner
2 loaves garlic bread
Large mushroom-and-pepperoni pizza
Large pitcher of beer
3 Milky Ways
Entire frozen cheesecake,
    eaten directly out of the freezer.

From: *The Joy of Stress,* by Pam Pettler
(Quill, NY 1984, page 47).

SELF-EVALUATION

Here is a list of some things that you studied in this chapter. How did you do on each item? Check your answers.

	I UNDERSTAND THIS PRETTY WELL	I LEARNED SOMETHING, BUT I NEED TO LEARN MORE	I DON'T UNDERSTAND THIS
I studied:			
how to understand menus and order food in restaurants	____	____	____
about restaurant customs	____	____	____
how to understand charts and interviews about healthful foods, exercise, and stress	____	____	____
how to give advice about health	____	____	____
how to hear the difference between *can* and *can't*	____	____	____
about people's habits and life styles 10,000 years ago	____	____	____
about some older people's advice on how to stay young	____	____	____

What's one thing that you would like to improve about your listening or speaking in the next chapter?

I'm going to work on . . .

_____

_____

Culture Shock

*T*his chapter has four parts. You'll listen to people explain culture shock and tell about their experiences with it. You'll discuss your own experiences and ways to get through culture shock. Look at this list of some of the things that you'll study in this chapter. What's most important for you to learn? Put a 1. What's next most important? Put a 2, etc.

I WANT TO LEARN:

A. about the different stages of culture shock _____

B. to follow directions in English _____

C. to relax _____

D. to guess the meaning of new words without a dictionary _____

E. to get the main idea when I listen or read even if I don't understand every word _____

F. about some North American customs _____

A. Listen to the song and answer the questions.

Sometimes I Feel Like A Motherless Child

Slowly

Some-times I feel like a moth-er-less child, _____

Some-times I feel like a moth-er-less child. __ Some-times I

feel like a moth-er-less child, A long way from home __

__ A long way from home. _____

Sometimes I feel like I'm almost
gone. (3)
A long ways from home, a long ways
from home.

Sometimes I feel like a feather in the
air. (3)
A long ways from home, a long ways
from home.

IT WORKS!
Learning Strategy:
Discussing Your
Feelings

1. How do you feel when you hear this song?
2. Do you sometimes feel like this when you're away from your
family, friends, or country?
B. You don't need to understand every word when you read. Sometimes
it's important just to understand the writer's mood (feeling). Read
the paragraphs and answer the questions.

READING 1

The city, in the rain, is a gray smudge against the hills. Strange. In
the summer, everything is bright white, and the tourists run around,
laughing and taking pictures. But now, in winter, there are no tourists,
and the whitewashed buildings are streaked with gray. The streets are
empty. People huddle indoors. They peer sadly out of windows, waiting,
waiting. What are they waiting for? I don't know. An occasional cat slips
wetly from under a parked car and slinks into a doorway. The cat watches
and waits, waits. But nothing happens. I think the rain will never stop.

—from the journal of an American student living in Europe

Threads

He that travels much
knows much.

Thomas Fuller

READING 2

I've decided to cook a big chicken soup. This sounds easy, but it's not. My problem is finding a chicken. Back in Vancouver, all the chickens are in plastic at the supermarket. They're all cleaned and cut up. But here, I can't find any that look like that. Here, the only chickens that I've seen are at the outdoor marketplace, and they're ALIVE. What am I going to do? How do people buy chickens here? I don't understand. Do I have to take a LIVE chicken home with me and kill it in my kitchen? Oh! I can't do that. Maybe the chicken man at the marketplace will kill it for me. But that doesn't seem much better. I don't want to ride home on the bus with a DEAD CHICKEN. I guess I'll have to take out my dictionary and practice: "Please take off the head, take off the feathers, and cut it up for me."

—from the journal of a Canadian student living in Asia

QUESTIONS

1. What is the mood of the first student? Why might the student feel like this? Do you sometimes feel like this?
2. What is the problem of the second student? What are some small problems that you have in this country?

PART ONE: UNDERSTANDING CULTURE SHOCK

Before You Listen

IT WORKS!
Learning Strategy:
Thinking Ahead
about a Subject

A. How do you feel about being in this country? Check your answers to the sentences below. Be honest!

QUESTIONNAIRE	YES	NO
1. I am excited and happy about my experiences in this country.	_____	_____
2. I feel like I'm beginning a new life.	_____	_____
3. I am often confused and unhappy in this culture.	_____	_____
4. I really prefer to spend time with other people from my country.	_____	_____
5. My new life here is terrible.	_____	_____
6. I'm beginning to understand this new culture.	_____	_____
7. I'm beginning to like some of the customs here.	_____	_____
8. I feel comfortable in this culture.	_____	_____
9. I feel like I belong in this culture.	_____	_____

B. You will hear a lecture about culture shock. For each word on the left, tell which expression on the right has the same meaning. Write the letter on the line.

_____ **1.** transition   **a.** not different; almost the same

_____ **2.** stage   **b.** change

_____ **3.** expert   **c.** very sad

_____ **4.** similar   **d.** person who knows a lot about a subject

_____ **5.** depressed   **e.** step; period of time

Listening

You're going to hear a lecture about the stages of culture shock. Read the boxes below before you listen. Then, as you listen, fill in the small boxes with the correct numbers (1, 2, 3, or 4). (Which happens first? Second? Third? Fourth?) Listen more than once if necessary.

IT WORKS!
Learning Strategy:
Associating

STAGE NUMBER ☐

People begin to feel comfortable in the new culture. They begin to like some customs and to make friends.

STAGE NUMBER ☐

People are excited and happy about the new culture. They're interested in everything.

STAGE NUMBER ☐

People are confused and angry or depressed. They spend a lot of time with people from their own country. This new culture is very strange to them, and simple things seem to be difficult. This is a very negative stage.

STAGE NUMBER ☐

People understand the new culture and have good friends. They feel very comfortable.

After You Listen

A. Read the paragraphs on pages 76-77 again. What stage of culture shock are these people in?

B. Look at your answers to the questionnaire on page 77. What stage of culture shock are you in?

C. With a small group (three to four people), give advice to people in Stage 2 of culture shock. These people are confused and depressed. What can they do to move on to Stage 3? What can they do to be happier? Use modals of advice (*should, shouldn't, ought to*) in your answers. (Choose a group secretary to write your answers.)

PART TWO: ADJUSTING TO A NEW CULTURE

Before You Listen

A. Think of the good and bad things about living in this country. Write them on the lines below.

B. Share your answers with a partner. Then share your answers with a small group. Add anything to your list that you want to.

GOOD	BAD
_____	_____
_____	_____
_____	_____
_____	_____
_____	_____
_____	_____
_____	_____
_____	_____

IT WORKS!
Learning Strategy:
Analyzing

IT WORKS!
Learning Strategy:
Brainstorming

C. You are going to hear two people talk about their experience with culture shock. Both people now live in the United States. Before you listen, guess the meanings of the underlined words in the sentences below.

1. I suffered from very <u>severe</u>—very serious—culture shock.

2. I felt so <u>homesick</u>! I thought a lot about my country, my family, my friends. I was really depressed, and I wanted to go back home.

3. Sometimes people in a new culture <u>associate</u> only with other people from their country. They don't want to spend time with people from the new culture.

4. I only felt <u>at ease</u>, I only felt comfortable, with people from my country.

5. They're citizens of Brazil. They live in Canada now, but they still have Brazilian <u>citizenship</u>.

6. When he was in high school, he came to the United States for one year as an <u>exchange student</u>. He lived with an American family and went to an American high school.

7. It was hard to <u>adjust</u> to a new culture. It wasn't easy to change my way of thinking.

Listening

A. Read the questions below. Listen to Person 1 and think about the answers as you listen. Listen more than once if necessary. Then answer the questions before you listen to the next speaker. Remember that you don't need to understand every word. Think about what you *do* understand. Don't worry about the other words.

1. Where is the speaker from?

2. Why did he first come to the United States?

3. What was his experience with culture shock?

4. What happened when he went back to his own country?

B. Read the questions below. Listen to Person 2 and think about the answers as you listen. Listen more than once if necessary. Then answer the questions.

1. Where is the speaker from?

2. Why did she come to the United States?

3. What was her experience with culture shock?

4. What did she do when she was homesick?

5. What happened when she went back to her country?

6. What did she decide to do?

LEARNING STRATEGY

Remembering New Material: If you put new words in the context of a situation, it helps you remember them.

After You Listen

GRAMMAR NOTE: PARTICIPLES AS ADJECTIVES

You can use many present and past participles as adjectives. Present participles end
in -ing. Most past participles end in -ed.

Present participles show the *cause*:	Past participles show the *effect*:
English is a *confusing* language.	I'm really *confused*.
The homework was *boring*.	The students were *bored*.

Here are some other common participles that you can use as adjectives:

depressing	depressed
exciting	excited
interesting	interested
irritating	irritated
shocking	shocked
tiring	tired

A. Complete the paragraph with words from the box "Participles as
Adjectives." In some sentences, there is more than one possible
answer.

When I first arrived in this country, I was really happy. I
was _____ (1) to be here. Everything was new
and _____(2). But then I started to have some
problems.   I had trouble with the language. A lot of the customs
were strange and _____(3). Some new customs
bothered me a little bit; they were just _____(4). But
others seemed really terrible. I was _____(5) by some
of them. I worked hard to learn the language. I spent five hours in
English class every day and two hours on homework. This was
very _____(6) so I didn't have much energy for other
things. Mostly, I was homesick. I missed my friends and family. I
stayed in my apartment all weekend and was _____(7).
    Slowly, things got better. I started to make friends and to go
places. My English got better. I began to understand the customs.
Now I'm _____(8) in life again, and I'm much happier.

B. In a small group, discuss your answers to these questions. (Use
participles and other adjectives.)
1. How did you feel when you first came to this country? What
seemed strange to you? What things did you notice?
2. How do you feel now? Which stage of culture shock are you in?
3. Is it possible to be in two stages at the same time? Is it possible to
stay in one stage forever?

C. How much do you already know about customs in this country? Take this quiz and find out!

QUICK QUIZ: SOME CUSTOMS IN NORTH AMERICA

1. Someone tells you, "That's a nice sweater." You say:
a. Thank you.
b. Oh, not really. It's very old.
c. Would you like it?

2. Your teacher sometimes sits on her desk. You think:
a. She's not polite.
b. She's not very serious about teaching.
c. It's not strange.

3. Someone has invited you to a party at 8:00. It's probably best to arrive:
a. a few minutes before 8:00.
b. at 8:00 exactly.
c. a few minutes after 8:00.

4. You have a business appointment for 10:30. It's probably best to arrive:
a. at 10:25 or 10:30.
b. at 10:35 to 10:45.
c. at 11:00.

5. You go out to lunch with an American friend. Who pays?
a. Your friend pays because lunch was his suggestion.
b. You both pay.
c. You pay because you're a little older than your friend.

6. Your American friend comes to your house for dinner. She has already eaten one serving of food. You say, "Would you like some more?" She says, "No, thank you. It was really delicious, but I'm so full!" What do you do?
a. Ask her two or three more times.
b. Say, "Are you sure? Well, if you change your mind, please help yourself."
c. Put some more food on her plate.

7. Last week, you had a short conversation with your American friend. He said, "Let's get together sometime for a movie or dinner or something. I'll give you a call." But he hasn't called. What do you think?*
a. Nothing is strange.
b. He isn't polite.
c. He hasn't called because he has a problem.

Note: There is more about this in Chapter 7

8. Your American neighbors are rich, but their two children (who are in high school) work part-time. One of them does babysitting on weekends. The other helps neighbors with the gardening on Saturdays. Your neighbors probably:
a. are bad parents.
b. care more about money than they care about their children.
c. love their children and are teaching them to be independent.

9. You tell your teacher, "I'm going to take the TOEFL exam tomorrow." Your teacher says, "Well. . ." and crosses two fingers (the index finger and the middle finger). You think that your teacher:
   a. is *very* impolite.
   b. is telling you "good luck."
   c. is angry because you're going to be absent.
10. You are taking a college history class. The person at the desk next to you looks like she is over fifty years old. Probably:
   a. This situation is very strange.
   b. She is waiting for her son or daughter, who is in the class.
   c. She has decided to go back to school; the situation isn't strange.

D. Share your answers with a small group. Which ones do you agree on? Which ones do you disagree on? Are you confused by any of them? Ask your teacher for his or her opinion.

E. Understanding your new culture can help you get through the difficult stage of culture shock. It's good to know the customs of another culture, but it's even better to know *why* people have those customs. Write a list of customs (from this country) that are confusing to you. You might choose some from the quiz on pages 82-83 or any others that confuse you. Then interview people at school or in your neighborhood. Tell them, "I find this confusing because I'm not American." And ask, "Why do people here do this?" Complete the chart below.

Threads

Don't judge a book
by its cover.

Proverb

IT WORKS!
Learning Strategy:
Developing Cultural
Understanding

Customs	Explanations
Example: People in this country usually say "thank you" after a compliment ("That's a nice sweater.").	They're thinking: "Thank you for saying that." It doesn't mean that they agree with the compliment.
_____	_____
_____	_____
_____	_____
_____	_____
_____	_____
_____	_____
_____	_____
_____	_____
_____	_____
_____	_____
_____	_____

PART THREE: LEARNING TO RELAX

Before You Listen

A. In Chapter 4 you listened to people talk about stress. Sometimes it's especially stressful to live in a new culture. What are some situations that make *you* nervous or tense? List them here.

_____   _____

_____   _____

B. Share your answers with a partner.

Listening

LEARNING STRATEGY

Understanding and Using Emotions: If you learn to relax, you enjoy the new culture more and develop language skills more easily.

You're going to do a relaxation exercise. Before you listen, take everything off your desk except a piece of paper and a pen or pencil. Then listen to the tape and follow the speaker's directions. Remember that it's okay to enjoy yourself in a language class!

After You Listen

Now You Choose. Do you feel more relaxed now? Without getting tense again, read the four writing topics below. Choose ONE of them. Then pick up your pen and begin to write. Don't worry about spelling or vocabulary. (If you don't know a word that you need, find a different, easier word. Or you can ask your teacher.) Put your writing in your portfolio.

1. In the relaxation exercise, you imagined a very beautiful place. Write one paragraph about this place. Describe the colors, sounds, and smells. How did you feel in this place?
2. Do you remember the student who had trouble finding a chicken for chicken soup (page 77)? Think of one problem that you have in this culture. Write one paragraph about it.
3. What is your experience with culture shock? What stage are you in? Are you homesick? If so, what are you doing about it? Write one paragraph about this.

4. Imagine that you have an American or Canadian friend who is going to live in your country for a few years. This person has never been there before and doesn't know anything about your culture. Write one paragraph of advice for your friend. What will probably be difficult for your friend in your country? What will be irritating or confusing or shocking? What should your friend do?

The Sound of It: Understanding Reductions

A. In normal or fast speech, you'll hear "reductions" of some words. Listen to these examples. Can you hear the difference between the long forms and the short forms?

LONG FORM	REDUCTION	SHORT FORM
She made a lot of friends.	lot of → lotta	She made a lotta* friends.
He had lots of problems.	lots of → lotsa	He had lotsa* problems.
He wasn't able to relax.	able to → able ta	He wasn't able ta* relax.
Could you help me with this?	could you → cudja	Cudja* help me with this?
I'll see you later.	you → ya	I'll see ya* later.
Do you know her?	her → er	Do you know er*?
Do you know him?	him → im	Do you know im*?
I was hurt and angry.	and → n	I was hurt n* angry.

These forms are not correct in writing.

B. Listen to these sentences. Do you hear a reduction? Check *Long Form* or *Short Form* as you listen

	Long Form	Short Form
a. She made a lot of friends.	✓	____
b. She made a lot of friends.	____	✓
1. They spent a lot of time with us.	____	____
2. Could you explain this?	____	____
3. Everything was new and exciting.	____	____
4. He had lots of new experiences.	____	____
5. After some time, I was able to enjoy the new culture.	____	____
6. Let's invite her.	____	____
7. Let's invite him.	____	____
8. I'll call you tomorrow.	____	____

C. Listen to these conversations. You'll hear reduced (short) forms. Write the long forms.

1. A: Do you know _____?

   B: Yeah. She's in my history class.

   A: _____ introduce me to _____?

2. A: I'm sick _____ tired of feeling like a foreigner.

   B: I know what you mean. There are a _____ problems in the beginning, but things will get better.

3. A: Where's Bill? Didn't you invite _____?

   B: Yeah, but he wasn't _____ come.

PART FOUR: A CROSS-CULTURAL STORY

Before You Listen

Threads

A good traveler is one who does not know where he is going to, and a perfect traveler does not know where he came from.

Lin Yutang

A. You're going to listen to (and read) a short story by William Saroyan. Saroyan was an American writer who lived in Fresno, California until his death in 1981. He came from a big Armenian family, so he had "one foot in each culture." In other words, he was both American and Armenian. He spoke English and Armenian. He understood the customs of both cultures. Many of his stories are about the two cultures.

When people live in another country, they have new experiences and learn new customs. They adjust to the new culture. They feel comfortable with their own customs, of course, but they also like some customs from their new country. They begin to choose the customs to follow—some old, some new.

Which customs from your culture are very important to you? Which customs from your new country are you beginning to like and feel comfortable with? Write them here.

CUSTOMS THAT I LIKE FROM MY COUNTRY	CUSTOMS THAT I LIKE FROM THIS COUNTRY
_____	_____
_____	_____
_____	_____
_____	_____
_____	_____
_____	_____

B. The story takes place on a train. There are some words for train travel. Complete the sentences with the words below.

aboard   aisle   smoker (= smoking car)
uniform   journey   diner (= dining car)
bumped into

Trains don't have smoking cars these days. Now there are bar cars.

1. The _____ from Fresno to New York was very pleasant. He enjoyed the trip a lot.

2. He got _____ the train in Fresno. Several days later, he got off the train in New York.

3. On the train, he walked down the _____ and looked for his seat.

4. He went to the _____ for lunch.

5. He went to the _____ to have a drink and play a game of poker (cards).

6. He was walking down the aisle when the train suddenly began to stop. A

   young woman _____ him. "Oh, excuse me," she apologized.

7. A man who was wearing a _____ checked their tickets. Then another conductor came to help him.

C. Before you listen, guess the meanings of the underlined words in the sentences below.

1. She asked me a question, but I <u>ignored</u> her. I didn't pay any attention to her.

2. He told everyone that he was a doctor, but later we found out that he was an <u>impostor</u>. He was only <u>pretending</u> to be a doctor, but he wasn't really one at all. Now he's in prison!

3. He seemed to me like an <u>amiable</u> young man. I thought he was friendly, but my uncle didn't like him.

4. You'll have to speak very loudly because he's almost <u>deaf</u>.

5. My mother used to serve tea every day at 4:00. She poured the tea, my sister served little sandwiches, and my brother served the cake. We all discussed the news and had our tea. It always happened the same way. But after the kids went away to college, my mother <u>abandoned</u> this <u>ritual</u>. She doesn't do it anymore.

D. In this story, an old man gives advice about travel to his nephew. What advice might you give someone before he or she takes a train trip?

E. Look at the pictures below. What's happening in each? Talk about these pictures with a partner.

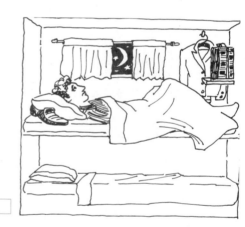

Listening

A. You are going to hear the story "Old Country Advice to the American Traveler," by William Saroyan. As you listen, read along silently. Don't worry about words that you do not understand. Instead, just concentrate on the main ideas.

B. When you finish, look at the pictures on page 88. Which pictures were in the old man's mind? (Put a 1 in those boxes.) Which pictures really happened? (Put a 2 in those boxes.) In some pictures, both might be correct.

OLD COUNTRY ADVICE TO THE AMERICAN TRAVELER

William Saroyan

One year my uncle Melik traveled from Fresno to New York. Before he got aboard the train his uncle Garro paid him a visit and told him about the dangers of travel.

When you get on the train, the old man said, choose your seat carefully, sit down, and do not look about.

Yes, sir, my uncle said.

Several moments after the train begins to move, the old man said, two men wearing uniforms will come down the aisle and ask you for your ticket. Ignore them. They will be impostors.

How will I know? my uncle said.

You will know, the old man said. You are no longer a child.

Yes sir, my uncle said.

Before you have traveled twenty miles an amiable young man will come to you and offer you a cigarette. Tell him you don't smoke. The cigarette will be doped.

Yes, sir, said my uncle.

On your way to the diner a very beautiful young woman will bump into you intentionally and almost embrace you, the old man said. She will be extremely apologetic and attractive, and your natural impulse will be to cultivate her friendship. Dismiss your natural impulse and go on in and eat. The woman will be an adventuress.

A what? my uncle said.

A whore, the old man shouted. Go on in and eat. Order the best food, and if the diner is crowded, and the beautiful young woman sits across the table from you, do not look into her eyes. If she speaks, pretend to be deaf.

Yes, sir, my uncle said.

Pretend to be deaf, the old man said. That is the only way out of it.

Out of what? my uncle said.

Out of the whole ungodly mess, the old man said. I have traveled. I know what I'm talking about.

Yes, sir, my uncle said.

Let's say no more about it, the old man said.

Yes, sir, my uncle said.

Let's not speak of the matter again, the old man said. It's finished. I have seven children. My life has been a full and righteous one. Let's not give it another thought. I have land, vines, trees, cattle, and money. One cannot have everything—except for a day or two at a time.

Yes, sir, my uncle said.

On your way back to your seat from the diner, the old man said, you will pass through the smoker. There you will find a game of cards in progress. The players will be three middle-aged men with expensive-looking rings on their fingers. They will nod at you pleasantly and one of them will invite you to join the game. Tell them, No speak English.

Yes, sir, my uncle said.

That is all, the old man said.

Thank you very much, my uncle said.

One thing more, the old man said. When you go to bed at night, take your money out of your pocket and put it in your shoe. Put your shoe under your pillow, keep your head on the pillow all night, *and don't sleep*.

Yes, sir, my uncle said.

That is all, the old man said.

The old man went away and the next day my uncle Melik got aboard the train and traveled straight across America to New York. The two men in uniforms were not impostors, the young man with the doped cigarette did not arrive, the beautiful young woman did not sit across the table from my uncle in the diner, and there was no card game in progress in the smoker. My uncle put his money in his shoe and put his shoe under his pillow and put his head on the pillow and didn't sleep all night the first night, but the second night he abandoned the whole ritual.

The second day he *himself* offered another young man a cigarette which the other young man accepted. In the diner my uncle went out of his way to sit at a table with a young lady. He started a poker game in the smoker, and long before the train ever got to New York my uncle knew everybody aboard the train and everybody knew him. Once, while the train was traveling through Ohio, my uncle and the young man who had accepted the cigarette and two young ladies on their way to Vassar formed a quartette and sang *The Wabash Blues*.

The journey was a very pleasant one.

When my uncle Melik came back from New York, his old uncle Garro visited him again.

I see you are looking all right, he said. Did you follow my instructions?

Yes, sir, my uncle said.

The old man looked far away in space.

I am pleased that *someone* has profited by my experience, he said.

After You Listen

IT WORKS!
Learning Strategy:
Making Inferences

A. Sometimes you don't need to know the exact meaning of a word. You only need to get the general idea.

1. The old man said: "Before you have traveled twenty miles an amiable young man will come to you and offer you a cigarette. Tell him you don't smoke. The cigarette will be doped."

You can guess that a *doped* cigarette:
a. is good.
b. is dangerous.
c. is expensive.

2. The old man said: ". . .a very beautiful young woman will bump into you intentionally and almost embrace you. She will be extremely apologetic and attractive. . . Go on in and eat. The woman will be an adventuress. . . A whore! . . . And if the diner is crowded, and the beautiful young woman sits across the table from you, do not look into her eyes. If she speaks, pretend to be deaf." You can guess that a *whore*:
   a. is good.
   b. is happy.
   c. is dangerous.

B. Before you came to this country, did someone (maybe your uncle, grandmother, or a family friend) give you advice? Did they say, "That's a dangerous country. You need to be very careful"? What advice did they give you? Talk about this in a small group.

*IT WORKS!
Learning Strategy:
Discussing Past
Experiences*

SELF-EVALUATION

This is a list of some things that you studied in this chapter. How did you do on each item? Check your answers.

	I UNDERSTAND THIS PRETTY WELL	I LEARNED SOMETHING, BUT I NEED TO LEARN MORE	I DON'T UNDERSTAND THIS
I studied:			
the stages of culture shock	_____	_____	_____
following directions in English	_____	_____	_____
how to relax	_____	_____	_____
guessing the meaning of new words without a dictionary	_____	_____	_____
getting the main idea	_____	_____	_____
North American customs	_____	_____	_____

Threads

In 1989, 2,066,510 people traveled between New York and San Francisco by airplane.

Air Transport 1990: The Annual Report of the US Scheduled Airline Industry

What's one thing that you would like to improve (or learn more about) in the next chapter?

I'm going to work on . . .

_____

_____

What Do You Mean? Thought and Communication

CHAPTER 6

*T*his chapter has three parts. You'll learn about some problems in communication—between men and women, between people on the phone, and between people and message machines. You'll learn how to solve some of these problems. Look at this list of some of the things that you'll study in the chapter. What's most important for you to learn? Put a 1. What's next most important? Put a 2, etc.

I WANT TO LEARN:

A. **about differences between men's and women's communication** ____

B. **how English speakers express emotion with intonation** ____

C. **to make an appointment** ____

D. **how to answer a negative question ("You're not going to the party?")** ____

E. **to get the main idea when I listen to someone even if I don't understand every word** ____

F. **to guess the meaning of new words without a dictionary** ____

G. **to understand people when they speak fast** ____

A. Look at the cartoon below. What does the artist believe about communication between men and women?

Reprinted by permission of Jeff MacNelly, San Jose Mercury News.

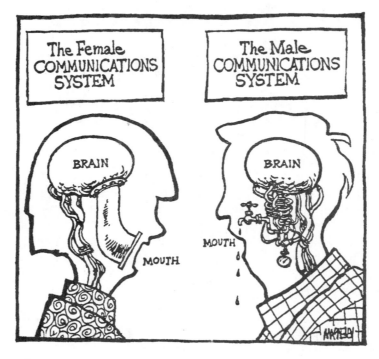

IT WORKS!
Learning Strategy:
Making Predictions

B. Where do communication problems begin? Here is a test. Scientists say that on this kind of test, men usually do better on Question 1. Women usually do better on Question 2. Take this test just for fun!

Question 1: Which picture (a, b, c, or d) is the same as the picture on the left?

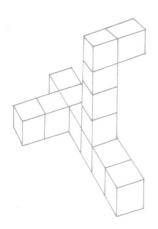

a.

b.

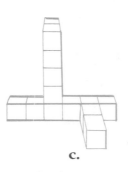

c.

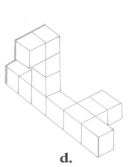

d.

Question 2: For one minute, look at the items in Box A. Then cover it up and look at the items in Box B. Cross out (X) anything that wasn't in Box A. How many items can you find?

A.

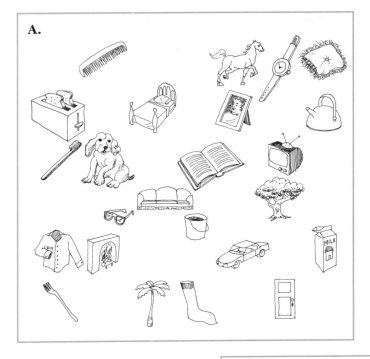

C. Think about how little boys and girls (in your culture) play and speak.
1. Do boys and girls usually play *together*—or boys with boys and girls with girls?
2. Are their games similar or different?
3. Who plays in large groups with a leader—boys or girls?
4. Who plays in small groups or with one other child—boys or girls?
5. Who probably has one "best friend"—boys or girls?
6. Who gives commands (for example, "Give me that!" or "Get out of here!")—boys or girls?
7. Who gives *suggestions,* not commands—boys or girls?
8. Who probably tells other children: "I'm better than you are"—boys or girls?

IT WORKS!
Learning Strategy:
Developing Cultural
Understanding

B.

Read this excerpt from a book by a linguist, Deborah Tannen. She is writing about children in American culture.

IT BEGINS AT THE BEGINNING

Deborah Tannen

Even if they grow up in the same neighborhood, on the same block, or in the same house, girls and boys grow up in different worlds of words. Anthropologists Daniel Maltz and Ruth Borker summarize research showing that boys and girls have very different ways of talking to their friends. Although they often play together, boys and girls spend most of their time playing in same-sex groups. Their favorite games are different, and their ways of using language in their games are separated by a world of difference.

Boys tend to play outside, in large groups. Their groups have a leader who tells others what to do and how to do it. Boys' games have winners and losers and systems of rules. Finally, boys frequently argue about who is best at what.

Girls, on the other hand, play in small groups or in pairs; the center of a girl's social life is a best friend. In their most frequent games, everyone gets a turn. Many of their activities (such as playing house) do not have winners or losers. Girls are expected not to show that they think they are better than the others. Girls don't give orders; they express their preferences as suggestions. Whereas boys say, "Gimme that!" and "Get outta here!" girls say, "Let's do this," and "How about doing that?" Much of the time, they simply sit together and talk.

Adapted from Deborah Tannen, *You Just Don't Understand* (New York, Ballantine Books, 1990), pages 43–44. Permission granted by ICM, Copyright © 1990 by Deborah Tannen.

DISCUSSION

1. Look at your predictions in Exercise C. Were your answers the same as Tannen's?
2. Were you surprised by anything in the reading?
3. Deborah Tannen was writing about children in the United States. Are children in your country similar or different?

PART ONE: MEN'S LANGUAGE AND WOMEN'S LANGUAGE

Before You Listen

A. You're going to listen to people talk about how men and women think and speak. Do they think and speak differently? Talk with as many people as possible—students in your class, other people at the school, and people in your neighborhood. (Talk with the same number of men and women.) Ask them one question: "Who talks more—men or women?" What do men believe? What do women believe? Count their answers and complete the chart below. You can use lines: ⫲⫲ = 5 people, for example)

QUESTION	MEN'S ANSWERS		WOMEN'S ANSWERS	
	Men talk more	Women talk more	Men talk more	Women talk more
Who talks more— men or women?	_____	_____	_____	_____

B. You are going to hear part of a talk by Deborah Tannen (an expert on language; and Helen Fisher (an expert on human culture).* Before you listen, guess the meanings of the underlined words in the sentences below.

1. She told us a funny *anecdote*. She knows a lot of these short, interesting stories.

2. There was one *couple* sitting on the couch. The husband was about forty years old, and his wife was a little younger.

3. My family is very *vocal*. Everyone in my family talks a lot.

4. He *complains* a lot. He's always saying, "This is a terrible situation," or "I'm so tired," or "I hate my job," or "She really bothers me."

5. I'd like to talk to you *in private*. I don't want other people to hear this.

6. *Intimacy* isn't always easy. Closeness to another person takes time, patience, and love.

7. If you want to *please* children, give them some ice cream. They'll be happy.

IT WORKS!
Learning Strategy:
Guessing

Listening

SECTION 1

A. Listen for the answer to this question: According to Deborah Tannen, who talks more—men or women?

IT WORKS!
Learning Strategy:
Getting the Main Idea

SECTION 2

B. Listen for the answers to these questions: According to Helen Fisher, how can men make women happy? How can women make men happy?

*From an interview with Deborah Tannen and anthropologist Helen Fisher on Modern Times with Larry Josephson. Used by permission.

After You Listen

A. Read the selection below and then answer the questions in the chart. Check *Men* or *Women*.

LOVE IS NEVER ENOUGH

Aaron T. Beck, M.D.

Daniel Maltz and Ruth Borker have summarized differences in the communication of men and women:

Asking questions. In male-female conversations, the female asks most of the questions. Women see questions as a way to keep a conversation going, while men see them as requests for information. Men think, *If she wants to tell me something, she'll tell me.* A woman thinks, *If I don't ask, he'll think I don't care.*

Showing closeness. Women show a greater use of the pronouns *you* and *we.* Men make more declarations of fact or opinion.

Many women feel, *The marriage is working as long as we can talk about it.* Husbands think, *The relationship is not working if we have to keep talking about it.*

Discussing problems upsets some husbands; they prefer to arrive at a quick, practical solution. But wives want to "talk the problem out."

—Adapted from Aaron T. Beck, *Love Is Never Enough* (New York: Harper & Row, 1988). Copyright © 1988 by Aaron T. Beck, M.D. Reprinted by permission of Harper Collins Publishers, Inc.

MALE-FEMALE CONVERSATION

In general . . .	Men	Women
Who asks most of the questions?	____	____
Who uses the words *you* and *we* a lot?	____	____
Who thinks "Questions keep a conversation going"?	____	____
Who asks questions when they want information?	____	____
Who makes more statements of fact or opinion?	____	____
Who prefers to talk about marriage problems?	____	____
Who doesn't like to discuss marriage problems?	____	____

B. In a small group (three to four students), discuss these questions.
   1. In your culture, do people complain: "Women talk too much, and men don't talk enough"?
   2. Deborah Tannen said that women talk a lot in private and men talk a lot in public. Is this true in your culture?
   3. Helen Fisher said, "If a man wants to please a woman, sit down and *talk* to her. And if a woman wants to get along with a man, she should *do* something with him." Do you agree with this?
   4. What do you like to talk about with your friends and family?
   5. What do you like to do with your friends and family?
C. What's a typical (usual, common) conversation that you have with your husband, wife, boyfriend, or girlfriend? Or what's a conversation that your parents often had? Write it and put it in your portfolio.

EXAMPLE: My mother: Oh, I had such a hard day at work! Everyone in the office is complaining about the new boss. I didn't even have time for lunch, and I'm so hungry! . . . So how was your day, dear?
My father: Okay.
My mother: Well, what happened at work?
My father: Nothing.

The Sound of It: Understanding Reductions

In normal or fast speech, you will hear reductions of some words. Listen to these examples. Can you hear the difference between the long forms and the short forms?

LONG FORM	REDUCTION	SHORT FORM
Get out of here.	out of → outta*	Get outta* here.
Give me that book.	give me → gimme*	Gimme* that book.
Let me ask you something.	let me → lemme*	Lemme* ask you something.
I don't know.	don't know →dunno*	I dunno.*
You like it, don't you?	don't you → doncha*	You like it, doncha?*
You liked it, didn't you?	didn't you → didncha?*	You liked it, didncha*

These forms are not correct in writing.

A. Listen to these sentences. Do you hear a reduction? Check *Long Form* or *Short Form* as you listen.

	LONG FORM	SHORT FORM
EXAMPLES:		
a. *Let me* help you.	✓	____
b. *Let me* help you.	____	✓
1. I *don't know* him.	____	____
2. *Give me* a minute, will you?	____	____
3. *Don't you* believe it?	____	____
4. I took it *out of* the closet.	____	____
5. We *don't know* her.	____	____
6. *Let me* talk with him.	____	____
7. *Give me* your opinion.	____	____
8. You believed it, *didn't you*?	____	____

B. Listen to these conversations. You'll hear reduced (short) forms. Write the long forms.

1. A: _____ talk with him about how you feel?
   B: Well, I tried to, but he doesn't like to discuss problems. I _____ why.

2. A: _____ the ball!
   B: No! This is our game. You get _____ here!

3. A: _____ think there's a problem?
   B: Yeah, well, maybe. _____ just think about it for a while.

PART TWO: EXPRESSING EMOTION

Before You Listen

Here are some sentences that men say in the listening passage. Are these emotional situations or not? What do you think?

EXAMPLES: Beautiful sunrise, dear.
That's a very sexy swimsuit.
Tickets for the Olympics?
This is the happiest day of my life.

Say these sentences out loud. What do you think the intonation should be? How will the men show their enthusiasm (excitement)?

Listening

As you listen, decide which pictures belong with the words. Put checks in the boxes.

1. "Beautiful sunrise, dear."

☐ ☐

2. "That's a very sexy swimsuit."

☐ ☐

3. "Tickets for the Olympics?"

☐ ☐

4. "This is the happiest day of my life."

☐ ☐

The Sound of It: Understanding Intonation

In English, people show emotion with intonation. When they are enthusiastic (excited) or very happy, their voices go up on stressed words. There are more "mountains" and "valleys" in their speech:

IT WORKS!
Learning Strategy:
Practicing

It's really wonderful.

When people are *not* very enthusiastic or happy, their voices don't usually go up. In the example below, the person *says* "It's really wonderful," but probably doesn't truly think so:

It's really wonderful.

When a person likes another person and wants to be friendly, the voice usually goes up:

Oh, hi. How are you?

When a person does not feel very friendly toward another person, the voice does not usually go up:

Oh, hi. How are you?

A. Listen to these sentences. Are the speakers enthusiastic or friendly or not? Check your answers.

	NOT VERY ENTHUSIASTIC OR FRIENDLY	ENTHUSIASTIC OR FRIENDLY
1. Good morning.	_____	_____
2. Good morning.	_____	_____
3. Yeah, I like it.	_____	_____
4. Yeah, I like it.	_____	_____
5. It was a good movie.	_____	_____
6. It was a good movie.	_____	_____
7. Is this for me?	_____	_____
8. Is this for me?	_____	_____
9. It's good to see you.	_____	_____
10. It's good to see you.	_____	_____

B. When a person shows quiet sincerity (honest, true feelings) the voice might not go up much, but there is probably a small pause between words or word groups.

EXAMPLE: He . . . is a great . . . friend.

When the person is not very sincere, there is usually no pause.

EXAMPLE: He'sagreatfriend.

Listen to these sentences. Are the speakers sincere or not? Check your answers.

	SINCERE	NOT SINCERE
1. This is a wonderful meal.	_____	_____
2. This is a wonderful meal.	_____	_____
3. I had a good time.	_____	_____
4. I had a good time.	_____	_____
5. We're very glad to see you.	_____	_____
6. We're very glad to see you.	_____	_____
7. She is a really special person.	_____	_____
8. She is a really special person.	_____	_____

C. Sometimes people's intonation is enthusiastic and sincere, but they don't really feel that way. How do you know? You can watch the expressions on their faces or listen to their other words.

EXAMPLE: I really want to marry you. Please pass the salt.

Listen to these conversations. After each conversation, you will hear a question. Choose the correct answer. Circle a, b, or c.

IT WORKS!
Learning Strategy:
Making Inferences

1. a. He thinks it's terrible.
   b. He truly thinks it's a great color.
   c. He isn't really interested.

2. a. He thinks it's terrible.
   b. He truly thinks it's a great color.
   c. He isn't really interested.

3. a. She thinks it was sad.
   b. She thinks it was truly funny.
   c. She thinks it wasn't very funny or interesting.

4. a. She thinks it was sad.
   b. She thinks it was truly funny.
   c. She thinks it wasn't very funny or interesting.

After You Listen

In a small group, discuss this question: In your culture, how do you know if a person is enthusiastic, friendly, or sincere?

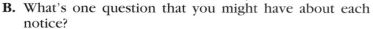

PART THREE: DEALING WITH COMMUNICATION PROBLEMS

Before You Listen

A. You are going to hear three telephone conversations about some of the notices below. These are all from a college bulletin board. Read the notices. If you don't understand something, ask other students. (If nobody understands, ask your teacher.)

B. What's one question that you might have about each notice?

FOR SALE

For sale: Toyota Tercel, 1985; well maintained and serviced regularly. Air conditioning. High-quality stereo, cassette player, sunroof. Runs great. $3750. Call Sarah, 555-9436.

For sale: 19" color TV. Excellent condition. Call Greg, 555-6211.

Learn Spanish. Native speaker. $15 per hour. All levels. Call Alvaro, 555-9948.

LESSONS

Piano lessons wanted. Need a piano teacher for beginning lessons on weekends. Call 555-7261.

Wanted: Chinese student to practice Chinese with. Will help with English in exchange. Call Alex, 555-1770

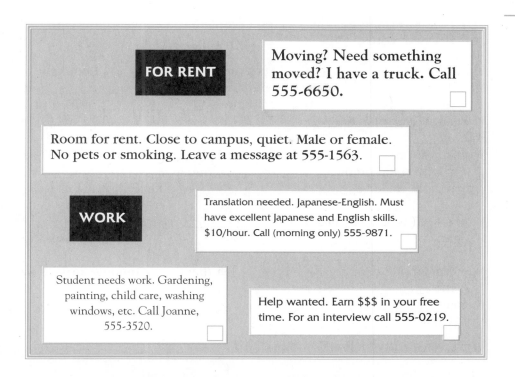

FOR RENT

Moving? Need something moved? I have a truck. Call 555-6650.

Room for rent. Close to campus, quiet. Male or female. No pets or smoking. Leave a message at 555-1563.

WORK

Translation needed. Japanese-English. Must have excellent Japanese and English skills. $10/hour. Call (morning only) 555-9871.

Student needs work. Gardening, painting, child care, washing windows, etc. Call Joanne, 555-3520.

Help wanted. Earn $$$ in your free time. For an interview call 555-0219.

Listening

A. Listen to the three conversations. Write the number of the conversation (1, 2, or 3) in the box next to the notice that goes with it.

B. Listen to Conversation 1 again and answer these questions.

How long has the woman been teaching?

Can she give lessons at the man's house?

C. Listen to Conversation 2 again. Complete this form with the man's message.

Time: _____
While You Were Out
_____ called.
Telephone Number: _____
☐ returned your call
☐ wants to see you
☐ please call back
☐ will call again
☐ other
Message: _____
_____
_____

D. Listen to Conversation 3 again. Complete the conversation with the stressed words.

Woman: Good _____. Start time _____ Company.

Man: Hello. I'm _____ about your help _____ ad at the _____. Uh, what kind of _____ is it?

Woman: Well, you'd be _____ _____ fliers.

Man: _____? Could you _____ more about that?

Woman: We're _____ a new _____ theater. We need you to stand on the _____ and give _____ to people walking _____—you know, to advertise the _____.

Man: Oh, okay. Could I make an _____ for an _____?

Woman: Yes, of _____. How's _____ morning at _____?

Man: I'm afraid I have a _____ at that time. Could we make it in the _____?

Woman: _____. How about _____?

Man: Great.

After You Listen

A. Write one or two notices for your class bulletin board or for a class "newspaper." These can be serious or funny. Do you want to sell something or buy something? Do you need to find a roommate? Do you want to take lessons or give lessons? Put it in your notice!

MAKING APPOINTMENTS

When you make an appointment, both speakers need to agree on the time. What can you say if the other person suggests a time that is not possible for you? You can say several different things. Here's an example from the top of the page.

EXAMPLE:

A: Could I make an appointment for an interview?

B: Yes, of course. How's Tuesday morning at 10:00?

A: I'm afraid I have a class at that time. Could we make it in the afternoon?

B: Sure. How about 3:00?

A: Great.

Don't be shy about asking for a different time or day!

B. Work with a partner. Look at the conversation on page 107. One student is A, and one student is B. Take roles and have a conversation. Choose words from the lists. Then change roles and have another conversation. Choose different words from the lists.

A: Could I make an appointment   { for an interview?
 with a counselor?
 with the doctor?

B: Yes, of course.   How about
 How's
 We have an opening on   }   { Tuesday at 10:00?
 Friday at 3:00?
 the 14th at 9:00?

A: I'm afraid
 Oh, I'm sorry, but   }   { I have a class at that time.
 I can't make it that day.

       Could we make it   { another time?
 a little later?
 a different day?

B: Oh, sure.   { How about Thursday?
 How's that same day at 4:00?
 We can fit you in on Friday afternoon.

A: Great. See you then.

C. Work with a partner. Student A wants to make an appointment with the dentist. Student B is the dentist's receptionist (secretary). Student A uses the calendar below. Student B uses the appointment book on the next page. Have a conversation. Use some of the expressions from exercise **B**.

Student's Calendar

Sunday 9	*picnic 11:30*	
Monday 10	*class 9—12*	*work 1—5*
Tuesday 11	*class 1—4*	
Wednesday 12	*class 9—12*	*work 1—5*
Thursday 13	*meet J. 10:00*	*class 1—4*
Friday 14	*class 9—12*	
Saturday 15	*movie w/ S!*	

Dentist's Appointment Book

Monday   10

9:00–10:00	*Ann Evans —teeth cleaning*
10:00–11:00	
11:00–12:00	*F. Dale—check-up*
closed for lunch	
2:00–3:00	*Marian Forbes—extractions*
3:00–4:00	
4:00–5:00	*E. Chavez-check-up*

Tuesday   11

9:00–10:00	*Bill Wong*
10:00–11:00	
11:00–12:00	
closed for lunch	
2:00–3:00	
3:00–4:00	
4:00–5:00	*N. Sarkisian—cleaning*

Wednesday   12

9:00–10:00	
10:00–11:00	
11:00–12:00	
closed for lunch	
2:00–3:00	*conference with Dr. Allen*
3:00–4:00	
4:00–5:00	

Thursday   13

9:00–10:00	*G. Porter—check-up*
10:00–11:00	
11:00–12:00	*M. Forbes—fit for denture*
closed for lunch	
2:00–3:00	
3:00–4:00	
4:00–5:00	*Ed Cohen–fill cavity*

Friday   14

9:00–10:00	*L. Miles—cleaning*
10:00–11:00	*meet w/ Dr. Fahmian*
11:00–12:00	
closed for lunch	
2:00–3:00	
3:00–4:00	
4:00–5:00	

D. Now change roles. Student A is the dentist's receptionist, and Student B wants to make an appointment. Have another conversation.

E. After you finish, write one of your conversations. Your teacher may want you to present it to the class or put it on tape. Put it in your portfolio.

The Sound of It: Understanding Intonation in Negative Questions

People often use statement word order to ask a negative question if they think the answer will be "no." Their intonation goes up. Here's an example from Conversation 1.

EXAMPLE: Question: You don't have one?

In many languages, people answer "yes" because they're thinking, "Yes, that's right. I don't have one." But in English the answer is "no."

EXAMPLE: Question: You don't have one?
Answer: No (I don't).

*IT WORKS!
Learning Strategy:
Practicing
Conversations*

A. With a partner, take turns asking and answering these questions. In each case, answer "no" and give the correct answer. Then listen and check your answers.

EXAMPLE: **a:**   The main language of Quebec isn't English?

   b: _No, it's French_   (French)

1. a: It's not strange to experience culture shock?

   b: _____ (normal)

2. a: Osaka isn't the capital of Japan?

   b: _____ (Tokyo)

3. a: Men don't usually talk much at home?

   b: _____ (in public)

4. a: Women don't usually talk much in public?

   b: _____ (at home)

5. a: English isn't easy?

   b: _____ (hard)

6. a: You're not from Canada?

   b: _____

B. You show surprise in a negative question if your intonation goes down low and then up high at the end.

EXAMPLE: Question: You don't have one?

Answer: No, I don't.

With a partner, take turns asking and answering these questions. Person A will show surprise in the question. Person B will answer "no" and add a short negative answer. Then listen and check your answers.

EXAMPLE: **a:** The main language of Quebec isn't English?

b: *No, it isn't.*

1. a: We don't have class tomorrow?

b: _____

2. a: You didn't see it?

b: _____

3. a: He doesn't like it?

b: _____

4. a: They won't even try it?

b: _____

5. a: She hasn't studied English before?

b: _____

6. a: You're not from around here?

b: _____

C. Sometimes a person thinks that the answer to a question will be "no," but that person isn't right. How do you answer?

EXAMPLE: Question: You don't have one?

Answer: Yes, I *do.*

It's very important to stress the affirmative verb in the answer (*do* in the example).

Ask and answer Questions 1-6 from Exercise B (above). This time Person B will answer "yes" and correct Person A.

D. Now You Choose. Choose *one* of the writing topics below either Using Telephone Answering Machines *or* Discussing Business on the Phone.

USING TELEPHONE ANSWERING MACHINES

1. Use a cassette recorder. Practice recording a short message for your answering machine. (For an example, listen again to Conversation 2.)
2. Call movie theaters and listen to the messages. Find out about three movies.

Theater: _____

Movie: _____

Times: _____ Price_____

Theater: _____

Movie: _____

Times: _____ Price_____

Theater: _____

Movie: _____

Times: _____ Price_____

Theater: _____

Movie: _____

Times: _____ Price_____

3. Pretend that you are calling a friend. Your friend isn't home, so you need to leave a message. Use a cassette recorder. Practice recording a short message for your friend. Invite your friend to one of the three movies.

DISCUSSING BUSINESS ON THE PHONE

1. Work with a partner. Choose two notices from pages 104–105 that look interesting—one for you and one for your partner.
2. Have two conversations. For one, call your partner. For the other, your partner will call you. Talk about the notices.
3. After you finish, write one of your conversations. Then record it on a cassette tape and put it in your portfolio.

SELF-EVALUATION

Here is a list of some things that you studied in this chapter. How did you do on each item? Check your answers.

	I UNDERSTAND THIS PRETTY WELL	I LEARNED SOMETHING, BUT I NEED TO LEARN MORE	I DON'T UNDERSTAND THIS
I studied:			
about the differences between men's and women's communication	_____	_____	_____
how English speakers express emotion with intonation	_____	_____	_____
how to make an appointment	_____	_____	_____
how to answer a negative question	_____	_____	_____
getting the main idea	_____	_____	_____
guessing the meaning of new words without a dictionary	_____	_____	_____
understanding fast English	_____	_____	_____

What's one thing that you would like to improve about your listening or speaking in the next chapter?

I'm going to work on . . .

_____

_____

_____

_____

Love, Marriage, and Friendship

*T*his chapter has four parts. You'll listen to people talking about meeting people, getting to know them, falling in love, and staying in relationships. And you'll give your own ideas about relationships. Look at this list of some of the things that you'll study in this chapter. What's most important for you to learn? Put a 1. What's next most important? Put a 2. etc.

I WANT TO LEARN:

A. to relax and enjoy a story in English without
understanding every word   _____

B. to make invitations and suggestions in English   _____

C. the difference between serious invitations and
polite expressions that aren't serious invitations   _____

D. how to accept or decline invitations   _____

E. to guess the meaning of new words without
a dictionary   _____

F. how to ask personal questions in a polite way   _____

G. to organize and give a speech   _____

A. Read the cartoon and the line by William Shakespeare and answer the questions.

"The course of true love never did run smooth."
—William Shakespeare, Much Ado About Nothing, Act I, Scene I, line 134.

QUESTIONS

IT WORKS!
Learning Strategy:
Discussing Your
Feelings

1. How does the man want to spend $50?
2. How does the woman want to spend $50?
3. What does the man think about the woman's list?
4. What does the woman think about the man's list?
5. Look at the last picture. (A *driving range* is a place to practice golf. A *therapist* is a psychologist—a person who helps people by talking with them.) Why does the man need to go to the driving range? Why does the woman need to go to the therapist?
6. How would *you* like to spend $50? List six possibilities.

_____   _____

_____   _____

_____   _____

7. When you're upset (angry, depressed), what do you do? Do you talk about your problem with someone? Do you do something (such as play a sport or work in the garden)?
8. Read the line by Shakespeare again. It means, "Love isn't easy." What do you think? Do you agree? Give an example.
B. Read the list on page 115 and answer the questions. The list tells how American men want to "fix" (change, improve) women and how American women want to "fix" men.

MEN FIXING WOMEN	WOMEN FIXING MEN
Women "should":	Men "should":
talk less	talk more
be less emotional	be more emotional
be more physical	be less physical
be less "romantic"	be more "romantic"
want more sex	want less sex
be less involved with others' problems	care more about people
laugh less	lighten up, be silly
be more rational	be more spontaneous
be more serious	have more fun
put job/career first	put family first
stay home more	go out of the home more
change less	be more flexible
have less attention on clothes	have more attention on how they dress
spend less time getting ready	have more attention on personal hygiene
be less sensitive	be more compassionate
be on time	be more flexible with time

—Joe Tanenbaum, *Male and Female Realities* (Sugar Land, Texas: Candle Publishing Company, 1989), p. 18.

1. This list was written about Americans. Which items on the list are true for your culture?

2. Which items do you agree with?

PART ONE: MEETING PEOPLE

Before You Listen

A. Imagine this situation: You're walking down the street. You see a *very* attractive person. You would like to get this person's attention—to meet him or her. What can you say or do?

_____

_____

IT WORKS!
Learning Strategy:
Thinking Ahead about
a Subject

B. Look at the picture. Write these words below it on the correct lines.

shop   parking meter
briefcase   Cadillac convertible
pocket   sidewalk
dime

C. Answer these questions about the picture.
   1. What is happening in the picture?
   2. Whom does the man notice?
   3. What is the man thinking?
   4. What will he do?

Listening

You are going to hear a famous American storyteller, Garrison Keillor,* tell about an experience on a New York street. Don't worry if you don't understand ever word. If you can relax and laugh, you'll enjoy your new language more and learn faster. As you listen, think about the answers to these questions:

What did the man do? Why?

What did the woman do?

Note: *to lean against* = to stand against

Used by permission of Garrison Keillor. Copyright © 1984 by Garrison Keillor.

After You Listen

IT WORKS!
Learning Strategy:
Brainstorming

Work in a group of four to five students. Discuss this question: What are different ways to meet someone? Make a list of all the group's ideas. The ideas can be serious or silly. Choose one person to be the group's "secretary." This person will write everyone's ideas.

PART TWO: INVITATIONS

Before You Listen

People in any relationship (friendship, love, or business) need to know how to make invitations and how to respond to (answer) them. Work with a partner. How do people make invitations in English? Think of as many ways as you can. Write them here.

_____

_____

_____

_____

_____

_____

Listening

IT WORKS!
Learning Strategy:
Making Inferences

A. You are going to hear four conversations. In each one, someone invites another person to do something. Don't worry if you don't understand every word. Just listen for the answer to this question: Which are serious invitations? If you're not sure, put a question mark.

	SERIOUS INVITATION	NOT A SERIOUS INVITATION
Conversation 1	_____	_____
Conversation 2	_____	_____
Conversation 3	_____	_____
Conversation 4	_____	_____

MAKING INVITATIONS OR SUGGESTIONS

There are two kinds of invitations and suggestions in English: *specific* and *general*.

SPECIFIC	GENERAL
Can you come to dinner next Friday at 8:00?	Why don't we get together sometime soon?
Would you like to go to a movie tomorrow night?	Let's have dinner or something in a couple of weeks.

Specific invitations are serious. The speaker really wants to get together and needs an answer. General invitations are friendly expressions but not very serious. The two people might or might not get together. You need to listen for words or expressions that are specific and words and expressions that are general.

SPECIFIC	GENERAL
next Saturday	sometime
tomorrow morning	in a couple of weeks
this evening	sometime soon
at 7:30	one of these days
on May 24th	some day

B. Listen to these sentences. Are they serious invitations? Check *Serious* or *Not very serious*.

	SERIOUS	NOT VERY SERIOUS
1.	_____	_____
2.	_____	_____
3.	_____	_____
4.	_____	_____
5.	_____	_____
6.	_____	_____
7.	_____	_____
8.	_____	_____

C. Turn back to page **117**. Listen again to the four conversations. Were your answers correct?

After You Listen

ACCEPTING AND DECLINING INVITATIONS

How do you answer an invitation? If the invitation is *general,* you accept it (say "yes") in a general way.

EXAMPLES: That sounds good.
Sure. Good idea.
Great. I'll give you a call.
Okay. I'll call you.

If the invitation is *specific,* you need to answer in a specific way. If you want to accept, ask for or give a specific time or place in your answer.

EXAMPLES: That sounds good. *What time* do you want to meet?
Sure. Good idea. *Where* should we meet?
Great. I'll give you a call *tonight.*
Okay. I'll call you *tomorrow morning.*

If you want to decline (say "no"), you need to tell the person "no" and say a few more words to be polite.

EXAMPLES: No, I'm sorry. I'm busy that night.
Oh, I can't do it that day. I have an appointment.
No, I can't make it then. Maybe another night?
No, that's a bad day for me. But let's get together soon.

Work with a partner. Practice invitations. One person will make an invitation. The other person will accept or decline. Then change roles. Use some of these words:

IT WORKS!
Learning Strategy:
Practicing
Conversations

Making an invitation:

Why don't we . . . Can you . . . Would you like to . . .	have a cup of coffee see a movie go to a game	next weekend? sometime soon? on Friday night?
Let's	get together have lunch	some day. one of these days.

Accepting an invitation (specific or general):

That sounds good.
Sure. Good idea.
Great. I'll give you a call.
Okay. I'll call you.

Accepting a specific invitation:

What time . . . ?
Where . . . ?
. . .this evening.
. . .tomorrow morning.
. . .on Thursday.

Declining a specific invitation:

No, . . .
- I'm sorry.
- I can't make it then.
- that's a bad time for me.
- I'm busy that day.

Maybe another day?
But let's get together soon.

PART THREE: LONGTIME LOVE

Before You Listen

> The heart that loves is
> always young.
> —*Greek proverb*

A. Answer these questions.
  1. What is Valentine's Day? How do people celebrate it in North America? (If you aren't sure, ask your teacher.)
  2. Do you celebrate Valentine's Day in your country? If so, how?
  3. Do you know anyone who has been married for many years?
  4. Do you know anyone who got married when they were old?
B. You're going to hear two couples talk about their marriages.* Before you listen, guess the meanings of the underlined words in the sentences below.
  1. My grandparents had true, <u>lasting</u> love. They never stopped loving each other.
  2. On their first <u>date</u>, my parents went to a concert and dinner. It was very romantic!
  3. There weren't enough chairs, so the child sat on her father's <u>lap</u>.
  4. She's a <u>widow</u>. Her husband died several years ago.
  5. The widow went to a <u>grief counselor</u> for help because she was so depressed in her widowhood. This therapist helped her feel better.

IT WORKS!
Learning Strategy:
Guessing

Listening

SECTION 1

A. Listen to the first couple, the Higginbothems, and answer these questions. Listen several times if necessary. Don't worry if you don't understand every word. Just listen for the information you need.

1. When did this couple meet?

_____

2. Why did they go to Grand Junction for one of their dates?

_____

3. Mr. Higginbothem remembers something that Mrs. Higginbothem doesn't remember. What is it?

_____

4. How many Valentine's Days have they spent together?

_____

_____

IT WORKS!
Learning Strategy:
Listening for Details

Threads

About 25% of all married women are older than their husbands.

SECTION 2

B. Listen to the second couple, the Baldwins, and answer these questions. Listen several times if necessary. Don't worry if you don't understand every word. Just listen for the information you need.

1. What did Mrs. Baldwin do when she was a grandmother?

_____

_____

2. What was Mrs. Baldwin writing about?

_____

_____

3. How did the Baldwins meet?

_____

_____

4. When the Baldwins got married, what did Mrs. Baldwin's mother say?

_____

_____

5. What did Mrs. Baldwin's mother do when she was 83 years old?

_____

_____

IT WORKS!
Learning Strategy:
Getting Information

After You Listen

ASKING PERSONAL QUESTIONS

Sometimes you want to ask someone a personal (private) question, but it might not be polite to do this.

Before you ask someone a personal question, you need to say something else to make it more polite.

EXAMPLE: May I ask you a personal question?
Do you mind if I ask you something personal?
I have a question for you. You don't have to answer, but. . .

A. Talk with five people who are married. How did these people meet their spouses (husbands or wives)? Complete the chart below with their answers.

	WHERE?	IN WHAT SITUATION?
PERSON 1	_____	_____
PERSON 2	_____	_____
PERSON 3	_____	_____
PERSON 4	_____	_____
PERSON 5	_____	_____

Threads

Most Americans marry between the ages of 25 and 29.

IT WORKS!
Learning Strategy:
Organize Your Ideas

B. *Now You Choose.* Choose one of the topics below, either **A**, **B**, or **C**. Give a short oral (spoken) report to a small group or to the class. In your report you'll answer the questions. Follow these steps.
1. Brainstorm. Write quick notes of all your ideas.
2. Work on vocabulary. If you need some new words, ask a classmate, your teacher, or a friend—or use a dictionary.
3. Put your ideas in order. Discard (throw out) any ideas that don't belong.
4. Put notes on an index card.
5. Give your speech. When you speak, don't read from the index card. Just look at it a few times to remember your ideas.

a. In the United States, people often go back to school when they're old. Some people get married when they're old. What do you think about this? Does this happen in your country?

b. In your country, how do people meet people to marry? (Where? In what situations?) How did people find spouses in the past—fifty or a hundred years ago? Were the customs different from today? For example, how did your parents meet? How did your grandparents meet?

c. In your country, what happens on a wedding (marriage) day? What are two or three important wedding customs? Are these different now from customs in the past?

PART FOUR: A RADIO DRAMA

Before You Listen

A. You are going to hear an advertisement for a pasta company.* The ad is in the form of a radio drama. You won't hear much English because every word in the drama is a kind of pasta! Before you listen, think of as many kinds of pasta as you can. Write them on the lines below. Don't worry about spelling. (If you have an Italian student in class, this person can correct your spelling.)

KINDS OF PASTA

<u> capellini </u>   _____   _____

<u> vermicelli </u>   _____   _____

<u> rigatoni </u>   _____   _____

B. Share your answers with a small group. Add more words to your list.
C. Share your answers with the whole class. One person will put the words on the board.

Listening

Very often, you can understand more from people's intonation than from their words. Listen to the ad two or three times. As you listen, think about these questions:

- Who are the people?
- How do they feel about each other?
- What happens in this drama?

*RONZONI Pasta radio commercial is a courtesy of Hershey Food Corporation.

IT WORKS!
Learning Strategy:
Understanding Tone
of Voice

After You Listen

Work in groups or with the whole class. Play a bit of the tape, stop, and guess what the people were saying. Write it down. Play a bit more of the tape, stop, and write. Continue this way and write a conversation in English. There are no "correct" or "incorrect" answers. Just do this activity for fun.

The Sound of It: Listening for Stressed Words

A. Listen to these sentences and repeat them. Notice the stressed words.
   1. How ARE you?
   2. Let's get TOGETHER sometime.
   3. I'll give you a CALL.
   4. Let's have LUNCH sometime soon.
   5. What do you want to get MARRIED for?
   6. I was HOPING she would NOTICE.
   7. I'll be GLAD when final EXAMS are over.

B. Listen to the important (stressed) words in these sentences. Underline them. (Some sentences have two stressed words.)
   1. Who is that?
   2. May I ask you a question?
   3. I'm busy that night.
   4. I'll call you tomorrow morning.
   5. I have a question for you.
   6. That sounds good.

C. Work with a partner. Figure out which word(s) should be stressed *in the answers* below. Underline those stressed words. When you finish all five, listen to the tape to see if you were right. Then practice saying the questions and answers.
   1. Question: Where does she want to GO?
      Answer: She wants to go to a movie.
   2. Question: Where does SHE want to go?
      Answer: She wants to go to a movie.
   3. Question: What did they DO?
      Answer: They got married.
   4. Question: WHEN did they get married?
      Answer: They got married last year.
   5. Question: What TIME should we MEET?
      Answer: Let's meet at about 8:00.

Threads

Approximately 30% of American women never get married.

SELF-EVALUATION

Here is a list of some of the things that you studied in this chapter. How did you do on each item? Check your answers.

	I UNDERSTAND THIS PRETTY WELL	I LEARNED SOMETHING, BUT I NEED TO LEARN MORE	I DON'T UNDERSTAND THIS
I studied:			
relaxing and enjoying a story in English without understanding every word	_____	_____	_____
making invitations and suggestions	_____	_____	_____
the difference between serious invitations and polite expressions that aren't serious invitations	_____	_____	_____
how to accept or decline invitations	_____	_____	_____
guessing the meaning of new words without a dictionary	_____	_____	_____
asking personal questions in a polite way	_____	_____	_____
organizing and giving a speech	_____	_____	_____

Threads

People who live together before marriage are 33% more likely to get a divorce.

What's one thing that you would like to improve about your listening or speaking in the next chapter?

I'm going to work on . . .

_____

_____

Advertising . . .
and Shopping

*T*his chapter has six parts. You'll hear some American radio advertisements and find out some practical things about shopping in a place where people speak English. Look at this list of some of the things that you'll study in this chapter. What's most important for you to learn? Put a 1. What's next most important? Put a 2, etc.

I WANT TO LEARN:

A. **how to use the yellow pages of the telephone book** ____

B. **how to understand messages on answering machines** ____

C. **how to make a purchase** ____

D. **how to express wants and preferences** ____

E. **how to return something to a store** ____

F. **how to express agreement and disagreement** ____

G. **how to understand incomplete sentences and short answers to questions** ____

Look at the pictures and read the information.

"Advertisers use mainly a few themes again and again: happiness, youth, success, status, luxury, fashion, and beauty. They hide class differences and problems in the workplace. Many ads suggest that you can solve all human problems by buying things. . . . They suggest that modern things are good and traditional things are bad. Today, more advertisers are directing their ads toward the poor in Third World countries. Even poor families, when living together . . . can have a total household income of more than $10,000 a year. . . . As one ad professional said, 'Once the TV set goes to work, the family is like a kid in a candy store. They watch 450 commercials a week. They see all the beautiful things. And they want everything that they see.'"

Adapted from Noreene Janus, *Cultural Survival Quarterly* (Summer 1983).

"The meaning in most people's lives comes much more from what they use than from what they produce in their jobs. Clothes, furniture, records, all the things that we buy involve decisions and the use of our own choice. . . . Shopping is a social event. . . . It makes you feel normal. Most people find it cheers them up—even window shopping."

Adapted from Judith Williamson, *Consuming Passions: The Dynamics of Popular Culture* (London and New York; Marion Boyards, Ltd., 1986).

Here is an American car with a bumper sticker about shopping. Here are some other bumper stickers about shopping:
•A woman's place is in the mall (shopping center).
•If you think money can't buy happiness, you've been shopping in the wrong places.
•More is more.
•When the going gets tough, the tough go shopping.
•Shopping is my Everest.

QUESTIONS

1. What are some of the themes that advertisers use?
2. What do many advertisements suggest?
3. What happens when poor people see ads on television?

DISCUSSION

1. Do you like to go shopping? Does it "cheer you up" (make you happy)?
2. Do you go window shopping when you don't have money to buy things?
3. What kinds of things do you like to shop for? What kinds of things do you *not* like to shop for?

IT WORKS!
Learning Strategy:
Discussing Your
Feelings

PART ONE: UNDERSTANDING ADVERTISING; USING THE YELLOW PAGES

Before You Listen

A. Have you ever looked at the yellow pages of your telephone book? They give you a lot of useful information. Here are some examples of things that you can look up in the yellow pages.
- barber shops
- beauty salons
- bicycles
- computers
- pharmacies
- restaurants
- shoes
- sporting goods

The yellow pages have an index that shows where to look for the item you need. Then you look on the page the index gives you. Here is a section of an index. If you want to rent a car, what page would you look on? Circle it.

> Car Radios—See
>   Automobile Radios & Stereophonic Systems 123
> Car Rental—See Automobile Renting 124
> Car Telephone—See Cellular Telephones 260

Threads

Phone books in the United States have a lot of useful information in them: what to do in an emergency, community services, information about postal services and public transportation, information about shopping, recreation, government offices, and, of course, how to use telephone services.

B. Below are four ads from the yellow pages of four different telephone books (for different cities). For each ad, find the following information:
- What is the advertisement for?
- Is there an address for the business?
- What is the address of the business?
- What is the telephone number of the business?

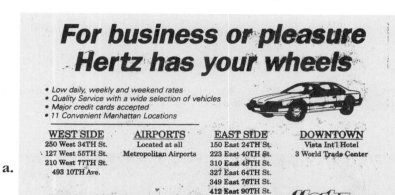

a.

For business or pleasure Hertz has your wheels

- Low daily, weekly and weekend rates
- Quality Service with a wide selection of vehicles
- Major credit cards accepted
- 11 Convenient Manhattan Locations

WEST SIDE	AIRPORTS	EAST SIDE	DOWNTOWN
250 West 34TH St.	Located at all	150 East 24TH St.	Vista Int'l Hotel
127 West 55TH St.	Metropolitan Airports	223 East 40TH St.	3 World Trade Center
210 West 77TH St.		310 East 48TH St.	
493 10TH Ave.		327 East 64TH St.	
		349 East 76TH St.	
		412 East 90TH St.	

Worldwide Reservations call toll free dial
"1" & then **800 654-3131**
Hertz rents Fords and other fine cars
HERTZ RENT A CAR

Hertz
AMERICA'S WHEELS

b.

STANFORD DRIVING SCHOOL

RELAXED METHOD

RECOGNIZED BY EDUCATORS AS THE BAY AREA'S FINEST

INTERNATIONAL STUDENTS WELCOME
BRUSH-UPS TOO!

ACCELERATED TEENAGE
DRIVER EDUCATION AND TRAINING

- DEFENSIVE DRIVING TECHNIQUES
- DUAL CONTROLS/AIR CONDITIONED
- FREE HOME PICK UP
- FREE 1 HR. ADULT PERMIT TRIP
- BONDED AND INSURED - PL & PD
- DMV #2520

FOR YOUR LESSONS
PLEASE CALL

415 493-1978

c.

SAVE TIME EFFORT & MONEY
LET US PLAN YOUR
"SUPERTRIP"
SUPERTRIP

YOUR FIRST CLASS TRAVEL AGENCY
FULL QUALITY SERVICE FOR:
VACATIONS - GROUP TRAVEL - CORPORATE TRAVEL

DOMESTIC & INTERNATIONAL
AIR - HOTEL - LAND - SEA
ALL COMPUTERIZED RESERVATIONS
ALL MAJOR CREDIT CARDS

FAX: 213-382-6130 • TOLL FREE 800-338-1898

213-382-9688

3727 W. 6th ST., SUITE 318, L.A. 90020

d.

THERE'S NO BETTER WAY TO STAY IN TOUCH.℠

- Car phones, portables & transportables
- Clear reception & transmission
- Affordable pricing plans
- Sales, Service & Installation
- Automatic service in hundreds of cities
- Exclusive 'Follow Me Roaming' service

BellSouth Mobility
A *BELL*SOUTH COMPANY

© 1990 BellSouth Mobility

Corporate Headquarters 5600 Glenridge Dr. NE	24-Hour Customer Service	Sales Information	Local Sales Office 120 Interstate North Pkwy E	Local Sales Office 114 Southfield Pkwy Forest Park
847-3600	847-2400	847-3700	980-4100	362-5700

C. You will hear two radio advertisements. Before you listen, guess the meanings of the underlined words in the sentences below.

1. My friend Kim <u>volunteered</u> to take me to the bus station. I didn't ask her, but she offered.

2. I was in an automobile accident last week and got a <u>whiplash</u>. I really hurt my neck when the car stopped suddenly.

3. Because of the accident and the whiplash, I have to wear a <u>neck brace</u> to support my head.

4. Many modern buildings are made of <u>concrete</u>; concrete is hard and strong like stone, but it's much cheaper.

5. When I bought the ticket, I got a student <u>discount</u>, so I paid less.

Listening

A. You will hear two advertisements. There may be words in them that you don't understand. The first time you listen, just try to identify the business. Look at the ads from the yellow pages on page 130. Which yellow page ad is for the same business as the ad you hear? Write a, b, c, or d.

Ad 1: _____

Ad 2: _____

B. Listen again and answer the questions.
Ad 1: What does Doris need to do? Why?
Ad 2: What does Fred, the driving instructor, *not* want to do? What is he using?

*IT WORKS!
Learning Strategy:
Getting the Main Idea*

After You Listen

Get a copy of your local telephone book. (If you don't have one at home, ask your teacher for one or go to a public telephone.) Find a business for each of the items below. Write the name, address, and telephone number of the business.

1. a copy shop

Name of Business: _____

Address: _____

Telephone: _____

2. soccer or tennis balls

Name of Business: _____

Address: _____

Telephone: _____

3. a pharmacy that is open at night

Name of Business: _____

Address: _____

Telephone: _____

4. a place to have clothes cleaned (cleaners)

Name of Business: _____

Address: _____

Telephone: _____

5. a pizza restaurant that delivers (brings the pizza to you)

Name of Business: _____

Address: _____

Telephone: _____

6. a place to get a haircut

Name of Business: _____

Address: _____

Telephone: _____

7. a place to rent a piano or other musical instrument

Name of Business: _____

Address: _____

Telephone: _____

8. a bank

Name of Business: _____

Address: _____

Telephone: _____

PART TWO: UNDERSTANDING MESSAGES ON HOME ANSWERING MACHINES

Before You Listen

A. Do you have an answering machine on your phone? Do any of your friends have answering machines? In pairs, make a list of things you might hear on an answering machine that is in someone's house.

1. _____

2. _____

3. _____

B. For each expression on the left, tell which expression on the right has the same meaning. Write the letter on the line.

_____ **1.** croissant   **a.** to talk very loudly, yell

_____ **2.** to scream   **b.** Internal Revenue Service (which collects tax money)

_____ **3.** deaf   **c.** to be thankful for

_____ **4.** IRS   **d.** form that you return with your tax money

_____ **5.** to appreciate   **e.** not able to hear

_____ **6.** tax return   **f.** piece of bread or pastry in the shape of a crescent (half moon)

Listening

A. You are going to hear an advertisement for Arby's restaurants. Listen to the ad and answer these questions.
   • Who does the man from Arby's talk to?
   • What is Arby's advertising?
B. Listen to the ad again. What message does the man from Arby's leave?

After You Listen

Write a personal message for a home answering machine. Your teacher may want you to put it on tape. Put it in your portfolio.

_____

_____

PART THREE: UNDERSTANDING MESSAGES ON BUSINESS ANSWERING MACHINES

Before You Listen

Work in pairs. Look at the ad on page 134 for a bicycle shop from the yellow pages of the telephone book. What things do you think you might hear on a telephone message for this store? Make a list. Then compare your answers with one other student's.

IT WORKS!
Learning Strategy:
Making Predictions

1. _____

2. _____

3. _____

Listening

Listen to the message on the answering machine in the bicycle store. Answer the questions.

1. What days is the shop open?

   _____

2. During what hours is it open?

   _____

3. What is the location? El Camino and _____ (cross street)

After You Listen

*IT WORKS!
Learning Strategy:
Looking for Practice
Opportunities*

A. Look in the yellow pages of the telephone book for the number of a business or service that interests you. Call the store late in the evening or early in the morning. Is there a message on an answering machine? If so, what does it say? Take notes and share the information with the class.

_____

_____

_____

If there is no message, call the business during the day. Ask for the days and hours it is open and ask how to get there.

B. Many large organizations have long messages on their machines; the machines answer even during the day. The messages give instructions about what number to press on a touch-tone phone. For example, they may say: "Press 1 for hours, Press 2 for the address of the organization or directions to it, Press 3 for information about a certain topic," and so on. The message may then say, "For other information or if you are using a rotary phone, please stay on the line." (A rotary phone has a dial, not buttons you can press.) Examples of these organizations are the INS (Immigration and Naturalization Service), many large banks or companies that offer credit cards, airlines, and main offices of big businesses. Call a large organization with an answering machine. Take notes on the message and share the information with the class. (If you can understand the entire INS message, you should get an A+ for the week!)

C. Telephone quiz. On the left are some expressions that you might hear on the telephone. Match them with expressions on the right that have the same meanings.

1. The number you have dialed has been temporarily disconnected and is no longer in service.

    a. The person that you want is not at this number.

2. You can dial that direct.

    b. This is a taped message.

3. There is no one here by that name.

    c. This number is not "good" any more.

4. I have a collect call from Sue. Will you accept the charges?

    d. Will you pay for a call from Sue to you?

5. This is a recording.

    e. What number were you trying to call?

6. What number did you dial?

    f. You don't need an operator; you can make the call yourself.

Note: If someone calls you by mistake, you don't have to give your number. You can ask them what number they called and tell them, "Sorry, you have the wrong number."

CULTURAL NOTE

Did you know . . .?

Many large organizations have 800 numbers that you can call free, without paying. You can find out if a company has an 800 number by calling 1 800 555-1212 (the information operator for 800 numbers). You can get a directory of 800 numbers by contacting your local AT&T (American Telephone and Telegraph) office.

Before You Listen

Threads

People have three stages as consumers, or shoppers:

Young people want "possession experience"; they want to buy a house and fill it with objects.

Middle-age people spend money on things like travel, education, and sports.

Older adults want "being experiences"; they get the most happiness from simple pleasures and human contact.

A. You will hear a conversation in a store. Before you listen, guess the meanings of the underlined words in the sentences below.

1. I <u>recommend</u> that you buy a new computer—your old one is not working very well, so it would be a good idea to get another one.
2. There's a <u>sale</u> at the shopping center—let's go buy a new desk while the price is low.
3. They have other office <u>equipment</u> on sale too—like laser printers and fax machines.
4. I don't know how to use a computer. I hope my new computer comes with an <u>instruction manual</u> that is easy to read.
5. Do you pay <u>cash</u> for things you buy? Or do you charge them on your credit cards?
6. I always write <u>checks</u> to pay for things so that I have a record of what I spend.

EXPRESSING PREFERENCES AND WANTS

I want . . .	I'd prefer . . .
I'd like . . .	I'd rather have . . .

B. Work with a partner. You will hear a conversation in a store. A woman wants to buy a computer, and a salesclerk shows her different models. Then the woman buys a computer. What questions do you think the woman will ask? What questions will the salesclerk ask? Make lists.

QUESTIONS THAT THE WOMAN WILL ASK	QUESTIONS THAT THE SALESCLERK WILL ASK
1. _____ _____	1. _____ _____
2. _____ _____	2. _____ _____
3. _____ _____	3. _____ _____
4. _____ _____	4. _____ _____
5. _____ _____	5. _____ _____

Listening

A. Listen to the conversation at the computer store. As you listen, look at your list of questions above. Which questions does the woman ask? Which questions does the salesclerk ask? Check them on your list.

B. Listen to the conversation again. Look at your list of questions. Does the woman ask any questions that aren't on your list? Does the salesclerk ask any questions that aren't on your list? Add any new questions to your list.

C. You will hear an advertisement for Apple and Macintosh Computers. The ad is about two different kinds of buyers. You don't have to understand everything in the ad. Just listen to answer this question:
  • What is the difference between the two kinds of buyers?
  • Are you like Buyer 1 or Buyer 2?

IT WORKS!
Learning Strategy:
Practicing
Conversations

After You Listen

cathy®   **by Cathy Guisewite**

inedible = not eatable

IT WORKS!
Learning Strategy:
Practicing
Conversations

IT WORKS!
Learning Strategy:
Using Your
Imagination

A. Work with a partner. Have a conversation. One student is shopping in a store, and the other student is a clerk. The shopper asks several questions. The clerk answers the questions and tries to persuade the shopper to buy the product (you choose a product). Finally, the shopper buys the item. Your teacher may want you to present your conversation to the class or put it on tape. Put it in your portfolio. Note: You may want to use one of the products from the old-time ads below. If you do, imagine that you are living many years ago, 1900 for instance.

B. After you finish, write your conversation.

C. Imagine that you win a lot of money. You can buy anything that you want. What would you buy? Write a short description. Why would you buy it? Share your answer with a classmate and put it in your portfolio.

_____

_____

_____

_____

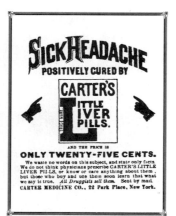

Before You Listen

You will hear an advertisement for AT&T communications. First, for each expression on the left, tell which expression on the right has the same meaning. Write the letter on the line.

_____**1.** reliable   **a.** warranty

_____**2.** to switch   **b.** dependable

_____**3.** guarantee   **c.** money that you get back

_____**4.** refund   **d.** safe, no-danger

_____**5.** no-risk   **e.** to change

Listening

Listen to the advertisement from AT&T communications and answer these questions:

- Who is Emerson?
- What idea does he give the boss (the head of the company)?

After You Listen

A. Work with a partner. Look at the conversation below. One student is A, and one student is B. Take roles and have a conversation. Choose words from the lists. Then change roles and have another conversation. Choose different words from the lists.

A: Hi, I'd like to return this $\begin{cases} \text{radio.} \\ \text{television set.} \\ \text{_____ (your idea).} \end{cases}$

B: What seems to be the $\begin{cases} \text{problem?} \\ \text{trouble?} \end{cases}$

A: It's $\begin{cases} \text{broken.} \\ \text{not working.} \\ \text{out of order.} \end{cases}$

B: Do you have the $\begin{cases} \text{guarantee?} \\ \text{warranty?} \end{cases}$

A: Of course, and I have the $\begin{cases} \text{receipt} \\ \text{sales slip} \end{cases}$ right here.

B: Well, I can $\begin{cases} \text{give you credit.} \\ \text{exchange it for you.} \end{cases}$

A: Thank you, but I'd prefer to get $\begin{cases} \text{my money back.} \\ \text{a refund.} \end{cases}$

Note: If what you return is clothing, you can give other reasons for returning it, especially if it was a gift that someone bought for you:

A: Hi, I need to return this $\begin{cases} \text{dress.} \\ \text{shirt.} \\ \text{pair of pants.} \end{cases}$

B: Why is that?

A: It's $\begin{cases} \text{the wrong color.} \\ \text{too big (small).} \\ \text{not the right size.} \end{cases}$

B. Have you ever returned anything to a store? What? What reason did you give for returning it? Did you get your money back? Did you get credit? Did you buy another item? Ask several people these questions. Write their answers in the chart below. Try to get at least three examples of items that people returned.

	ITEM	REASON FOR RETURNING IT	WHAT HAPPENED? (DID YOU GET A REFUND? CREDIT?)
Person 1	_____	_____	_____
	_____	_____	_____
Person 2	_____	_____	_____
	_____	_____	_____
Person 3	_____	_____	_____
	_____	_____	_____
Person 4	_____	_____	_____
	_____	_____	_____

IT WORKS!
Learning Strategy:
Getting Information

New Kind of Hat
Worn 10 Minutes a Day
Grows Hair
in 30 Days
~ or No Cost

How many people tried to return this?

Before You Listen

You are going to listen to an advertisement for Fox Television programming. The advertisement is about a woman who is in a big hurry to get home in time to see her TV shows (on the Fox weekend line-up on Channel WXIN-59). A policeman stops her for speeding (driving too fast). First, with a partner, answer these questions.

IT WORKS!
Learning Strategy:
Discussing Past
Experiences

1. Has a police officer ever stopped you (or a friend that you were driving with)? Why?
2. What did you do when the police officer stopped you? Did you pull over right away? Did you argue with the police officer? Did you get a ticket?

Listening

Listen to the following advertisement. There are some difficult words that you won't understand. Just listen and answer these questions:

- Does the woman argue with the police officer?
- Does he give her a ticket?

Note: *I bet you will.* = I think you will.
          to chat = to talk

142

After You Listen

A. Work with a partner. Have a conversation where people disagree, using *so, too,* and *not*. First, make short conversations following these examples:

EXAMPLES: I always watch public television.
You do not!
I do so (I do too)!

I never watch public television.
You do so (You do too)!
I do not.

1. I always listen to the radio news.
2. I love Crunchies cereal.
3. I never eat Crunchies cereal.
4. I always wear Guy's shoes.
5. I never wear Guy's shoes.
6. I always buy Powermilk Biscuits.
7. I never buy Powermilk Biscuits.

Have a conversation like one of the ones that you practiced, but use your own ideas. Your teacher may want you to present it to the class or put it on tape for your portfolio.

B. Work with a partner. Have a conversation where people agree. Use *too, either,* or *neither*. First, make short conversations following these examples:

EXAMPLES: I always watch public television.
I do too.

I never watch public television.
I don't either. (Neither do I.)

1. I always listen to the radio news.
2. I love Crunchies cereal.
3. I never eat Crunchies cereal.
4. I always wear Guy's shoes.
5. I never wear Guy's shoes.
6. I always buy Powermilk Biscuits.
7. I never buy Powermilk Biscuits.

Have a conversation like one of the ones that you practiced, but use your own ideas. Your teacher may want you to present it to the class or put it on tape for your portfolio.

C. After your finish, write your conversations.

The Sound of It: Understanding Incomplete Sentences

Understanding Incomplete Sentences: Sometimes people leave out (don't say) words because they know other people will still understand them. The words they leave out would not be stressed. If you know that sometimes people will leave out certain words, it will help your comprehension.

People leave out words more often in informal speech. In this chapter, you have heard many examples of this. Listen to these examples from this chapter.

EXAMPLE	COMPLETE SENTENCE
You ready, Doris?	Are you ready, Doris?
I'm not deaf—just not here.	I'm not deaf—I'm just not here.
We're open Saturday; closed on Sunday.	We're open Saturday; we're closed on Sunday.
You practice this?	Do you practice this?
Bet I will.	I bet I will.
If you already know what an Apple can do. . . I do.	If you already know what an Apple can do . . . I do already know what an Apple can do.
. . .and you're ready to buy one now . . . I am.	. . .and you're ready to buy one now . . . I am ready to buy one now.

Notice the last two examples: *I do. I am.* These are like short answers to *yes/no* questions. It is very common to answer a question with a short answer.

Grammar Note: Short Answers

SHORT ANSWERS TO *YES/NO* QUESTIONS		
With the verb *be:*	Yes, I am./No, I'm not.	Yes, he is./No, he's not (he isn't).
		Yes, they are./
		No, they're not (they aren't).
With the verb *do:*	Yes, I do./No, I don't. Yes, we do./No, we don't.	Yes, she does./No, she doesn't.
With *there is/are*:	Yes, there is./No, there isn't.	Yes, there are./No, there aren't.

A. Below are six questions and short answers. What words are missing in the answers? Write them in the blanks.

> EXAMPLE: Do you buy your food at ABC Market?
> Yes, I do (buy my food at ABC Market).

1. A: Is Koji home?

    B: Yes, he is (_____).

2. A: Do you want to go to the movies now?

    B: Yes, I do (_____).

3. A: Is there a movie on TV now?

    B: No, there isn't (_____).

4. A: Are you going shopping today?

    B: Yes, I am (_____).

5. A: Do they shop downtown?

    B: No, they don't (_____).

6. A: Do you need to go to the supermarket today?

    B: Yes, I do (_____).

B. You will hear six questions. For each question, circle the correct answer.

> EXAMPLE: Do they have a computer?
>
>   a. Yes, they are.　　　　(b.) Yes, they do.

1. a. Yes, I am.　　　　**b.** Yes, I do.

2. a. Yes, she does.　　　　**b.** Yes, she is.

3. a. No, he doesn't.　　　　**b.** No, he isn't.

4. a. No, I'm not.　　　　**b.** No, I don't.

5. a. Yes, there does.　　　　**b.** Yes, there is.

6. a. No, we aren't.　　　　**b.** No, we don't.

7. a. No, there aren't.　　　　**b.** No, there don't.

8. a. No, we're not.　　　　**b.** No, we don't.

"Any fool can make soap. It takes a clever man to sell it."

—*Thomas Barratt, of Pears' Soap.*
Ad from Christmas, 1897.

CULTURAL NOTE

Did you know . . .?

— Americans spend 40 to 50 percent of their income on housing and food.

— American women spend seven hours a week shopping, and American men spend five hours a week shopping; about half of the total time is for buying food and clothing.

— The average American home has two TV sets, six radios, a stereo, and a VCR. The TV is on seven hours a day, and the radio is on three hours a day.

SELF-EVALUATION

Here is a list of some things that you studied in this chapter. How did you do on each item? Check your answers.

	I UNDERSTAND THIS PRETTY WELL	I LEARNED SOMETHING, BUT I NEED TO LEARN MORE	I DON'T UNDERSTAND THIS
I studied:			
how to use the yellow pages of the telephone book	_____	_____	_____
how to understand messages on answering machines	_____	_____	_____
how to make a purchase	_____	_____	_____
how to express wants and preferences	_____	_____	_____
how to return something to a store	_____	_____	_____
how to express agreement and disagreement	_____	_____	_____
how to understand incomplete sentences and short answers to questions	_____	_____	_____

What's one thing that you would like to improve about your listening or speaking in the next chapter?

I'm going to work on . . .

_____

_____

What's in the News?

This chapter has four parts. You'll hear some weather reports, news stories, and other selections from TV or radio. Look at this list of some of the things that you'll study in this chapter. What's most important for you to learn? Put a 1. What's next most important? Put a 2, etc.

I WANT TO LEARN:

A. how to understand weather reports _____

B. how to describe weather _____

C. how to understand news headlines and stories _____

D. how to summarize a news story _____

E. how to understand numbers _____

F. how to express agreement and disagreement _____

Look at the pictures and read the information.

In 1989, Chinese students demonstrated for democracy in Tiananmen Square and other places in China. The government tried to hide information about the protests. "In America . . . Chinese students developed a new use for the fax machine—which of course works happily in any language. The students prepared news summaries and faxed them to many places in China with its one billion people. They had made history, and they knew it."

Adapted from Donald Wilhelm, *Global Communications and Political Power* (New Brunswick and London: 1990), pp. 119–20.

The Global Village

In 1991 Mikhail Gorbachev used electronic mail (computers) to communicate with the world when the Soviet military tried to take over his government. (He was under arrest and could not use the telephone.) This communication may have changed the world's history. Today many international organizations use fax machines and electronic mail for instant communication. In addition, home videotapes appear on TV news shows, and the video revolution makes it impossible for governments to decide what people should—or should not—see on their TVs. Even more important is the communication satellite, which sends messages through space instantly and is hard for governments to control. Says writer Danny Schechter: ". . . from Romania to South Africa to Tiananmen Square, it is no longer a question of whether we will see what the world sees, but when. Soon we'll be watching local and seeing global!"

Danny Schechter, "Watch Local, See Global," *Utne Reader* (July, August 1990), pp. 76–79.

QUESTIONS

1. What did Chinese students do in 1989?
2. How did Mikhail Gorbachev communicate with the world during the 1991 Soviet crisis?
3. How have communication satellites changed the news?
4. How do you get news? Do you watch TV? Listen to the radio? Read a newspaper or news magazine?

PART ONE: UNDERSTANDING WEATHER REPORTS

Before You Listen

A. Look at the pictures and read the weather expressions below.

It's sunny / warm / dry / fair.

It's cloudy / partly cloudy / overcast.

It's rainy. There are thunderstorms / scattered showers.

There's snow / ice.
It's freezing / icy.

It's cool / chilly / foggy.

It's windy / breezy.

B. Work with a partner. Look at the chart about U.S. weather and answer the questions.

Weather Close-Up

WEATHER/TRAVEL HOT LINE 1-900-555-5555 (Cost: 95¢ per minute) The 24-hour hot line gives touch-tone callers time, temperature, forecasts and travel conditions in 650 cities. Dial, then push "11" and the area code of desired city (selected area codes, left). For foreign weather and currency exchange rates: dial, push "11" and the first three letters of a city's name. FlightCall offers flight arrival, departure and gate information for airports with ✈ below, dial the 900 number and push "12." Have flight number. You must call from one of the metropolitan areas marked with a ✈. You can only get information for the major airport in that area.

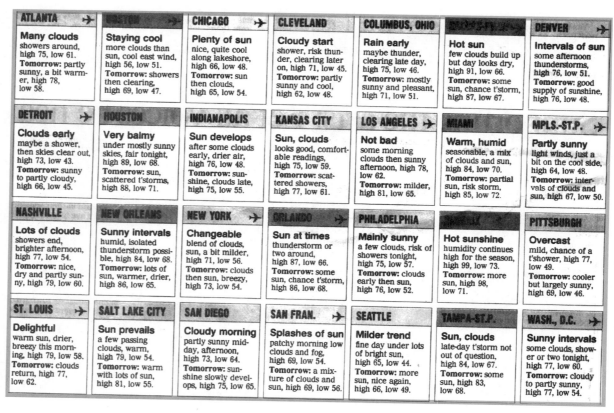

ATLANTA ✈	BOSTON ✈	CHICAGO ✈	CLEVELAND	COLUMBUS, OHIO	(city) ✈	DENVER ✈
Many clouds showers around, high 75, low 61. **Tomorrow:** partly sunny, a bit warmer, high 78, low 58.	**Staying cool** more clouds than sun, cool east wind, high 56, low 51. **Tomorrow:** showers then clearing, high 69, low 47.	**Plenty of sun** nice, quite cool along lakeshore, high 66, low 48. **Tomorrow:** sun then clouds, high 65, low 54.	**Cloudy start** shower, risk thunder, clearing later on, high 71, low 45. **Tomorrow:** partly sunny and cool, high 62, low 48.	**Rain early** maybe thunder, clearing late day, high 75, low 46. **Tomorrow:** mostly sunny and pleasant, high 71, low 51.	**Hot sun** few clouds build up but day looks dry, high 91, low 66. **Tomorrow:** some sun, chance t'storm, high 87, low 67.	**Intervals of sun** some afternoon thunderstorms, high 76, low 51. **Tomorrow:** good supply of sunshine, high 76, low 48.

DETROIT ✈	HOUSTON	INDIANAPOLIS	KANSAS CITY	LOS ANGELES ✈	MIAMI	MPLS.-ST.P. ✈
Clouds early maybe a shower, then skies clear out, high 73, low 43. **Tomorrow:** sunny to partly cloudy, high 66, low 45.	**Very balmy** under mostly sunny skies, fair tonight, high 89, low 68. **Tomorrow:** sun, scattered t'storms, high 88, low 71.	**Sun develops** after some clouds early, drier air, high 76, low 48. **Tomorrow:** sunshine, clouds late, high 75, low 55.	**Sun, clouds** looks good, comfortable readings, high 75, low 59. **Tomorrow:** scattered showers, high 77, low 61.	**Not bad** some morning clouds then sunny afternoon, high 78, low 62. **Tomorrow:** milder, high 81, low 65.	**Warm, humid** seasonable, a mix of clouds and sun, high 84, low 70. **Tomorrow:** partial sun, risk storm, high 85, low 72.	**Partly sunny** light winds, just a bit on the cool side, high 64, low 48. **Tomorrow:** intervals of clouds and sun, high 67, low 50.

NASHVILLE	NEW ORLEANS	NEW YORK ✈	ORLANDO ✈	PHILADELPHIA	(city)	PITTSBURGH
Lots of clouds showers end, brighter afternoon, high 77, low 54. **Tomorrow:** nice, dry and partly sunny, high 79, low 60.	**Sunny intervals** humid, isolated thunderstorm possible, high 84, low 68. **Tomorrow:** lots of sun, warmer, drier, high 86, low 65.	**Changeable** blend of clouds, sun, a bit milder, high 71, low 56. **Tomorrow:** clouds then sun, breezy, high 73, low 54.	**Sun at times** thunderstorm or two around, high 87, low 66. **Tomorrow:** some sun, chance t'storm, high 86, low 68.	**Mainly sunny** a few clouds, risk of showers tonight, high 75, low 57. **Tomorrow:** clouds early then sun, high 76, low 52.	**Hot sunshine** humidity continues high for the season, high 99, low 73. **Tomorrow:** more sun, high 98, low 71.	**Overcast** mild, chance of a t'shower, high 77, low 49. **Tomorrow:** cooler but largely sunny, high 69, low 46.

ST. LOUIS ✈	SALT LAKE CITY	SAN DIEGO	SAN FRAN. ✈	SEATTLE	TAMPA-ST.P.	WASH., D.C. ✈
Delightful warm sun, drier, breezy this morning, high 79, low 58. **Tomorrow:** clouds return, high 77, low 62.	**Sun prevails** a few passing clouds, warm, high 79, low 54. **Tomorrow:** warm with lots of sun, high 81, low 55.	**Cloudy morning** partly sunny midday, afternoon, high 73, low 64. **Tomorrow:** sunshine slowly develops, high 75, low 65.	**Splashes of sun** patchy morning low clouds and fog, high 69, low 54. **Tomorrow:** a mixture of clouds and sun, high 69, low 56.	**Milder trend** fine day under lots of bright sun, high 65, low 44. **Tomorrow:** more sun, nice again, high 66, low 49.	**Sun, clouds** late-day t'storm not out of question, high 84, low 67. **Tomorrow:** some sun, high 83, low 68.	**Sunny intervals** some clouds, shower or two tonight, high 77, low 60. **Tomorrow:** cloudy to partly sunny, high 77, low 54.

1. What's the weather like in New Orleans? Chicago? Washington DC?
2. What's the high temperature for the day in New York?
3. What's the low temperature for the day in Miami?
4. Is it going to rain in Columbus?
5. Is it going to be windy in Boston?

Grammar Note: Comparative and Superlative Adjectives

ADJECTIVE	COMPARATIVE	SUPERLATIVE
cold	cold**er**	cold**est**
dry	dri**er**	dri**est**
sunny	sunn**ier** (**more** sunny)	sunn**iest** (**most** sunny)
humid	**more** humid	**most** humid

C. Work with a partner. Look at the weather chart on page 152. Ask and answer questions about the weather in different places. Take turns. Compare cities.

EXAMPLES: What's the weather like in . . .
What's the high (low) in . . . ?
Is it sunny (cloudy, foggy, etc.) in . . . ?
Is it going to be foggier (rainier, colder) in San Francisco or Nashville?
Which city will have the hottest (coldest, windiest) day: San Francisco, Nashville, or Atlanta?

D. Look at the list of clothing items below. For each item, write the letter of the picture in the blank

_____ **1.** scarf

_____ **2.** snow boots

_____ **3.** rain boots

_____ **4.** heavy gloves

_____ **5.** umbrella

_____ **6.** raincoat

_____ **7.** overcoat

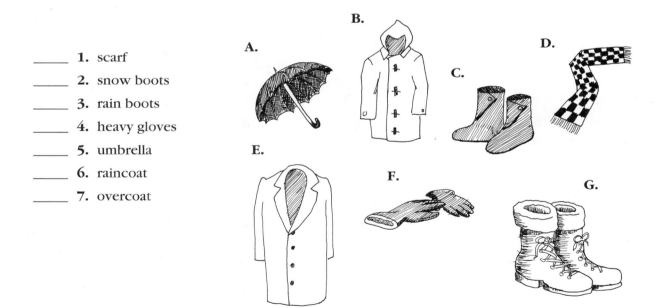

IT WORKS!
Learning Strategy:
Getting the Main Idea

Listening

A. You will hear four short weather reports from the morning news. For each report, tell what you would probably wear or take with you for the day. Use items from the list on page 153.

Weather Report 1: _____

Weather Report 2: _____

Weather Report 3: _____

Weather Report 4: _____

B. Listen again. For each report, tell the high and low temperatures the reporter gave.

Weather Report 1: _____

Weather Report 2: _____

Weather Report 3: _____

Weather Report 4: _____

Threads

Lightning strikes somewhere on earth about 6,000 times a minute.

IT WORKS!
Learning Strategy:
Listening for Details

After You Listen

A. Look at the chart on page 155 and answer the following questions.
   1. What was the high temperature in Cairo? Hong Kong? Tokyo?
   2. What was the low temperature in Bangkok? Singapore? Madrid?
   3. How many inches of precipitation (rain or snow) fell in Moscow? Guadalajara? Beijing?
   4. Which city had the hottest weather? Was that normal for the time of year?
   5. Which city had the coldest weather? Was that normal for the time of year?
   6. Which city had the most precipitation (rain or snow)?

Threads

A hurricane can release as much energy as 400 20-megaton H-bombs every second.

FOREIGN CITIES Following are the highest and lowest temperatures and daily precipitation (reported in inches) for the 24 hours ended 7 P.M. (E.D.T.) yesterday and the normal temperature range for this time of the year. *Not available. trc-trace.

Cities	Yesterday		Norm	Cities	Yesterday		Norm
Acapulco	93/75	0	90/ 73				
Amsterdam	63/52	0	57/ 48	Manila	*	0	93/ 75
Athens	73/55	1.0	75/ 59	Martinique	82/77	.02	88/ 73
Bangkok	101/84	0	95/ 77	Merida	86/59	.20	93/ 72
Beijing	77/55	.04	77/ 52	Mexico City	*	.08	79/ 54
Berlin	63/54	trc	63/ 45	Montego Bay	83/72	.24	86/ 75
Bermuda	78/72	0	73/ 64	Monterrey	74/66	0	86/ 66
Bonn	66/46	0	64/ 46	Montreal	62/39	0	61/ 41
Brussels	65/52	0	63/ 45	Moscow	65/48	0	63/ 45
Budapest	71/54	0	70/ 50	Nairobi	*	0	73/ 55
Buenos Aires	65/61	*	66/ 48	Nassau	80/70	.67	82/ 72
Cairo	87/75	0	90/ 61	New Delhi	*	0	104/ 75
Caracas	*	*	86/ 75	Nice	*	0	68/ 52
Casablanca	76/63	0	72/ 54	Oslo	64/39	0	54/ 36
Copenhagen	59/48	trc	57/ 43	Panama City	*	*	90/ 77
Dakar	77/68	0	82/ 66	Paris	72/43	0	64/ 46
Damascus	78/48	0	82/ 54	Prague	62/45	0	61/ 43
Dublin	58/50	trc	55/ 43	Rio de Janeiro	*	0	79/ 68
Edinburgh	57/54	trc	55/ 41	Riyadh	98/73	0	97/ 70
Edmonton	53/46	17	59/ 34	Rome	79/55	0	72/ 54
Geneva	*	0	64/ 46	Seoul	64/54	0	70/ 48
Guadalajara	79/59	.35	86/ 55	Shanghai	*	*	72/ 59
Havana	80/72	0	88/ 70	Singapore	87/75	0	90/ 75
Helsinki	58/43	.02	50/ 37	Stockholm	62/46	.12	54/ 39
Hong Kong	82/81	trc	81/ 72	Sydney	71/61	.02	68/ 54
Istanbul	66/50	0	68/ 52	Taipei	82/75	.01	81/ 68
Jerusalem	75/55	0	79/ 55	Tokyo	61/52	0	70/ 52
Johannesburg	75/54	0	68/ 45	Toronto	59/34	0	61/ 41
Kingston	90/79	0	88/ 75	Tunis	75/54	0	73/ 54
Lima	79/70	0	72/ 63	Vancouver	56/52	0	61/ 45
Lisbon	81/61	.02	70/ 55	Vienna	69/46	0	66/ 45
London	68/50	0	61/ 45	Warsaw	57/46	0	64/ 45
Madrid	77/46	.02	72/ 48	Winnipeg	70/46	0	61/ 36

B. What is the weather like in your home town? Are there four seasons (spring, summer, fall, winter) or two (rainy, dry)? What's the best time of year, in your opinion? The worst? Complete this chart about the "best" and "worst" seasons.

Home Town: _____

BEST SEASON

Months: _____

Weather: _____

_____

_____

What happens (what people do): _____

_____

_____

WORST SEASON

Months: _____

Weather: _____

_____

_____

What happens (what people do): _____

_____

_____

_____

C. Work with a partner. Look back at Chapter 2, Part One, making small talk. Very often people make small talk about the weather. Make small talk about today's weather in this situation:

SITUATION: You are at a bus stop. You have been waiting for the bus for a long time.

The Sound of It: Understanding Numbers

There are many situations where you will need to understand numbers, such as in prices, telephone numbers, or addresses. Learning to understand numbers will improve your listening comprehension in many circumstances. You heard numbers in the weather reports for temperatures.

A. Practice listening for ordinal numbers, which put things in order: *first, second, third, fourth, fifth,* and so on. Circle the number that you hear.

1.	14	14th
2.	20	20th
3.	21	21st
4.	32	32nd
5.	45	45th
6.	54	54th
7.	59	59th
8.	63	63rd
9.	67	67th
10.	78	78th

B. Practice listening to numbers that end in *-teen* and numbers that end in *-th*. Circle the number that you hear.

1.	13	13th
2.	14	14th
3.	15	15th
4.	16	16th
5.	17	17th
6.	18	18th
7.	19	19th

C. Practice listening to other numbers. Circle the number that you hear.

1.	13	30	30th
2.	4	14	4th
3.	5th	50	1st
4.	16	60	16th
5.	15	50	50th
6.	17	70	17th
7.	8	80	18th
8.	13	30	13th
9.	6	60	6th
10.	2	22	22nd
11.	9	19	9th
12.	17	70	70th
13.	14	40	40th
14.	9	90	90th

Before You Listen

A. Read the headlines of news stories below.

a. **AIDS increasing among teenagers**

b. **Rain forests in serious danger**

c. **Most cancer due to how we live, work**

d. **More people staying single and liking it**

e. **The smokeout: millions to quit smoking**

Most headlines do not have complete sentences. Here are the complete sentences for the headlines above.

AIDS *is* increasing among teenagers.
The rain forests *are* in serious danger.
Most cancer *is* due to how we live *and* work.
More people *are* staying single and liking it.
The smokeout: millions *of people will* quit smoking.

The words *a, an,* and *the* usually do not appear in headlines. Verbs like *is* and *are* often do not appear. *To* plus a verb usually means future (*be going to*): *Millions to Quit = Millions Are Going to Quit.* A comma sometimes appears instead of *and: live, work = live and work.*

B. Write the missing words in the headlines below.

EXAMPLE: Eastern Europe _____*Is*_____ Seeing More Tourists

1. More People _____ Avoiding Meat

2. Big Storm _____ to Arrive Tonight

3. _____ Japanese _____ Living Longer

4. Scientists _____ to Study _____ World's Warmer Weather

5. _____Chinese Diet _____ among _____ Healthiest

C. You will hear five news stories. Before you listen, guess the meanings of the underlined words in the sentences below.

   1. Experts say that the 55-mile-per-hour speed limit <u>prevents</u> accidents. There are fewer accidents when people drive more slowly.

   2. Which is more important—<u>heredity</u> or <u>environment</u>? Do our genes and physical characteristics—our heredity—determine who we are? Or does the situation or world that we live in—our environment—determine who we are?

   3. Each part of your body has thousands of small <u>cells</u>.

   4. I feel sick—I think I have a <u>virus</u> and am getting a cold or the flu.

   5. I tried to <u>quit</u> smoking, but I couldn't stop.

   6. My friend Emiko is a <u>researcher</u>. She's studying the effects of TV violence on children.

   7. She's making enough money to <u>support</u> herself, so she doesn't live with her parents anymore

   8. I don't need my old credit card, so I <u>destroyed</u> it—I cut it in half.

   9. <u>Tropical forests</u> have thousands of varieties of plants and animals in them, but the land is not good for agriculture.

  10. The president is having a <u>press conference</u> tonight to answer questions from reporters about the Middle East.

IT WORKS!
Learning Strategy:
Guessing

IT WORKS!
Learning Strategy:
Associating

Listening

A. Listen to the five news stories. Which news report goes with which headline? Write the letter in the blank.

News Report 1: ___*e*___

News Report 2: _____

News Report 3: _____

News Report 4: _____

News Report 5: _____

Threads

More people read newspapers in Europe and Japan. In the developing world, most people get their news from radio. In countries with average family size of four to five, television and radio are replacing newspapers as the main source of news information.

B. Listen to the stories again. Practice listening for numbers. Answer these questions:

1. News Report 1: How many people in the United States smoke?
   a. 15 million   **b.** 30 million   **c.** 50 million
2. News Report 2: How fast has the number of AIDS cases among U.S. teenagers grown in the past two years?
   a. 57 percent   **b.** 67 percent   **c.** 77 percent
3. News Report 3: Up to what percentage of all cancer might we be able to prevent?
   a. 60 percent   **b.** 70 percent   **c.** 80 percent
4. News Report 4: What percentage of men between the ages of 30 and 34 have never married?
   a. 25 percent   **b.** 30 percent   **c.** 35 percent
5. News Report 5: In how many years will we destroy the rain forests, at the present rate of destruction?
   a. 55 years   **b.** 105 years   **c.** 155 years

After You Listen

LEARNING STRATEGY

Summarizing: If you can summarize, you will be able to tell someone the important parts of a message quickly, without telling all the details.

A. Work in groups of five. Each person in the group chooses one of the news stories. (Each person should choose a different story.) Listen to the story again and take notes. Tell the group everything you can about the story. Other people in the group can ask questions. Write your notes here:

_____

_____

_____

IT WORKS!
Learning Strategy:
Looking for Practice
Opportunities

B. From now until the end of the class, watch two local and two national/international news programs a week in English. Your teacher can give you information about when you can see the news and on what channels. Complete the chart on the next page.

DATE	FIRST NEWS STORY MAIN IDEA	STORY THAT WAS MOST INTERESTING (SUMMARY)	VOCABULARY	QUESTIONS
_____	_____	_____	_____	_____
_____	_____	_____	_____	_____
_____	_____	_____	_____	_____
_____	_____	_____	_____	_____
_____	_____	_____	_____	_____
_____	_____	_____	_____	_____
_____	_____	_____	_____	_____

C. Choose a news story that made you especially happy or especially sad. Describe it to a partner. Your partner will ask you questions about the story. Tell why the story made you happy or sad.

PART THREE: SPECIAL REPORTS

Before You Listen

IT WORKS!
Learning Strategy:
Expressing Your
Feelings

For each expression on the left, tell which expression on the right has the same meaning. Write the letter on the line.

__b__ **1.** to cope   **a.** not nice, unkind

_____ **2.** somewhere else   **b.** to deal with (a problem)

_____ **3.** to play catch   **c.** to break, destroy

_____ **4.** best buddies   **d.** to throw and catch a ball (two or more people)

_____ **5.** mean   **e.** another place

_____ **6.** to shatter   **f.** very good friends

Listening

You are going to hear an ad for the Channel 3 Eyewitness News. Listen and answer the questions below. You may have to listen several times.
- A child is talking. What problem does she have?
- What will the subject of the news report be?

After You Listen

Look in a newspaper or TV magazine for a list of local TV programs. Find a news show or documentary about a current event or problem. Watch the show. Then complete this chart.

Name of program: _____

Day and time: _____

Subject: _____

What the program showed/What I learned: _____

_____

_____

_____

PART FOUR: VIOLENCE ON TV; DETERMINING POINT OF VIEW

Before You Listen

IT WORKS!
Learning Strategy:
Brainstorming

A. Work in groups. You will hear part of a conversation about violence on television. <u>Violence</u> is aggressive action or use of force. Before you listen, answer these questions:
1. What kinds of violence do you see on the news? Give examples.
2. What kinds of violence do you see in TV movies and shows? Give examples.
3. Do you watch violent programs on TV, or do you turn them off? Why?

B. In the conversation, there are some words that you may not know. Here are some of them:
<u>link</u> = connection
<u>I don't buy that.</u> (Slang) = I don't understand
<u>research</u> = studies by experts
<u>reflects</u> = shows
<u>to censor</u> = to cut something out of a book, magazine, TV show, etc. (usually because of an order from the government)
<u>censorship</u> = noun form of <u>censor</u>
<u>crisis</u> = a terrible situation
<u>the press</u> = journalists (reporters) from radio, TV, newspapers, etc.

Listening

A.   You will hear part of a conversation. Three people discuss their opinions about violence on TV. What do they think? Circle *Yes* or *No* for each person.

Question: Is there too much violence on TV? Does it cause violence in real life?

Person 1 (Tony):   yes   no

Person 2 (Nancy):   yes   no

Person 3 (Sue):   yes   no

B. Now listen to the conversation again. What do the three people think about censorship? Circle *Yes* or *No* for each person.

Question: Should there be laws to censor violence on TV in order to protect children?

Person 1 (Tony):   yes   no

Person 2 (Nancy):   yes   no

Person 3 (Sue):   yes   no

IT WORKS!
Learning Strategy:
Determining Point of
View

After You Listen

A.   Work with a partner. Read these expressions to agree or disagree with someone.

IT WORKS!
Learning Strategy:
Practicing
Conversations

Expressing Agreement and Disagreement

TO AGREE
Of course! Certainly! Sure! Naturally!
That's true. True.
That's right. Right.
That's a good point. I see your point. Good point.
I agree (completely).
I think so too.
You said it!
You're absolutely right.

TO DISAGREE
I disagree (completely). I don't agree (at all).
That's not true. That's not right.
That's ridiculous! What nonsense! (*not polite*)
I'm sorry to disagree, but . . .
I see your point of view, but . . .

Have a conversation. One of you wants to watch the news on TV. The other one wants to watch *Rambo 10* (or some other movie with a lot of violence). Express agreement or disagreement. Your teacher may ask you to present the conversation to the class or put it on tape for your portfolio.

IT WORKS!
Learning Strategy:
Getting Information

B. Read these statements:
1. It's better for children if parents divorce than if they live together and fight all the time.
2. People should not smoke in offices, schools, or other public places; it should be illegal (against the law).
3. Young people should have to ask their parents' permission before getting married.
4. Women should not be allowed in the military (army, navy, air force).
5. All people over the age of 18 should have to take a test for AIDS and learn the result.
6. There should be censorship of violence on TV to protect children.

Choose two of these statements. Ask at least five people in your class if they agree or disagree with each statement and why. Complete the charts.

STATEMENT NUMBER _____		
	Agree or Disagree	Why?
Person 1	_____	_____
Person 2	_____	_____
Person 3	_____	_____
Person 4	_____	_____
Person 5	_____	_____

Threads

Children in the United States see 26,000 murders on TV by the time they are 18 years old.

STATEMENT NUMBER _____

	Agree or Disagree	Why?
Person 1	_____	_____
Person 2	_____	_____
Person 3	_____	_____
Person 4	_____	_____
Person 5	_____	_____

C. Now you choose. Work with a partner. Choose one of the statements in Exercise **B**. Do you agree or disagree with it? Have a short conversation. Give reasons for your point of view. Your teacher may want you to present your conversation to the class or put it on tape. Write your conversation and put it in your portfolio.

SELF-EVALUATION

Here is a list of some things that you studied in this chapter. How did you do on each item? Check your answers.

	I UNDERSTAND THIS PRETTY WELL	I LEARNED SOMETHING, BUT I NEED TO LEARN MORE	I DON'T UNDERSTAND THIS
I studied:			
how to understand weather reports	_____	_____	_____
how to describe weather	_____	_____	_____
how to understand news headlines and stories	_____	_____	_____
how to summarize a news story	_____	_____	_____
how to understand numbers	_____	_____	_____
how to express agreement and disagreement	_____	_____	_____

What's one thing that you would like to improve about your listening or speaking in the next chapter?

I'm going to work on . . .

_____

_____

Planethood

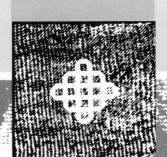

This chapter has three parts. You'll listen to people talk about environmental problems. You'll also talk about ways to solve these problems. Look at this list of some of the things that you'll study in the chapter. What's most important for you to learn? Put a 1. What's next most important? Put a 2, etc.

I WANT TO LEARN:

A. about environmental problems   ____
B. some possible solutions to environmental problems   ____
C. where many countries are on a world map   ____
D. to guess the meaning of new words   ____
E. to ask questions when I don't understand something   ____
F. to use a dictionary and choose the correct definition   ____
G. to work with other students to think of solutions to
    environmental problems   ____

A. Look at the photo and the world map. Read the information.

"I am a passenger on the spaceship Earth."

R. Buckminster Fuller, *Operating Manual for Spaceship Earth*

"The nation that destroys its soil destroys itself."

Franklin D. Roosevelt, letter to state governors, February 26, 1937

"We have forgotten how to be good guests, how to walk lightly on the Earth as its other creatures do."

Stockholm Conference, *Only One Earth,* 1972

B. Find your country on the world map. Draw in the borders and add the name of your country. You might need to write the name outside the map and draw a line to your country.

C. Do *one* of the following, task one *or* two::

   1. If there are students in your class from many different countries, exchange information with every student. Ask each one: "Where is your country?" Then add that student's country to your map. (Draw in the borders and write the name of the country.)

   2. The class breaks into five groups (1–5). Each group finds the countries for *one* of the groups below and puts them on the map.

IT WORKS!
Learning Strategy:
Identifying

GROUP 1	GROUP 2	GROUP 3	GROUP 4	GROUP 5
Afghanistan	Angola	Argentina	Brazil	Burma
Canada	Chile	China	Denmark	Egypt
Ethiopia	France	Germany	India	Greece
Japan	Kenya	Korea	Morocco	Iran
Nigeria	Poland	Russia	Spain	Mexico
Saudi Arabia	Turkey	United Kingdom (Great Britain)	U.S.A.	Venezuela

If you need help, ask each other or look at a book of maps (atlas). Then each student exchanges information with a student from each other group.

ATLANTIC OCEAN

PACIFIC OCEAN

INDIAN OCEAN

ARCTIC OCEAN

Before You Listen

LEARNING STRATEGY

Highlighting: If you mark new words or important ideas, you can easily find them again later.

A. You are going to hear six people answer this question: "What do you do to help the environment?" Before you listen, look at these pictures of environmental problems and read about them. Take a yellow (or pink or green) marking pen. Highlight (mark) the new words under the pictures.

Plastics are *not* biodegradable. They will remain in landfills for hundreds or thousands of years.

We burn oil, wood, and coal. This puts carbon dioxide (CO2) into the air. Usually trees and oceans absorb CO2, but now there's more than they can absorb. This causes the temperature of the earth to go up.

Many products (such as batteries, motor oil, detergent, and household cleaning chemicals) pollute the water and land. These toxic chemicals kill plants and make people sick.

Smog (air pollution) from factories and cars causes health problems such as lung cancer. "Acid rain" (a kind of air pollution) kills fish and plants in lakes and rivers.

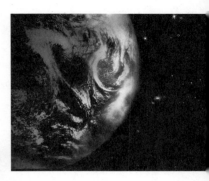

People are cutting down rainforests in Central and South America, Southeast Asia, and Africa. They want trees for wood or land for cattle (cows). Usually rainforests absorb CO_2, produce oxygen, and give us plants for medicine. But now we're cutting down 80 acres of forest every minute, a high price to pay for beef.

CFCs (from refrigerators, air conditioners, and white styrofoam cups) go into the atmosphere (air around the earth). Usually the ozone protects the earth from harmful (bad) sunlight. But CFCs are causing the ozone to get thinner. This causes skin cancer in animals and people.

B. Look for these words under the pictures. Guess their meanings. Match the meanings to the words. (Write the letters on the lines.)

1. _____ biodegradable
2. _____ air pollution
3. _____ landfill
4. _____ cattle
5. _____ atmosphere
6. _____ carbon dioxide
7. _____ to pollute
8. _____ ozone
9. _____ styrofoam
10. _____ CFCs
11. _____ acid rain
12. _____ temperature
13. _____ toxic chemicals
14. _____ to absorb

a. place for garbage
b. air around the planet
c. to make air, water, or land dirty and dangerous
d. a kind of plastic; we use it for plastic cups for hot drinks
e. a kind of air pollution
f. something in air conditioners and refrigerators
g. something that becomes part of the earth again, after some time
h. CO_2
i. heat or cold
j. something in the atmosphere that protects the earth from sunlight
k. poison
l. cows that people raise for meat
m. to take in or "drink" in
n. smog

Listening

On pages 170–171, there is a small box next to each picture. Listen to the six people talk about how they help the environment. Ask yourself, "Why do these people do these things? How—in small ways—are they helping?" For each person (1–6), choose a picture that shows the problem that they are helping to solve. Put a number (1–6) in the box next to the picture.

After You Listen

IT WORKS!
Learning Strategy:
Analyzing

A. Here are some environmental problems and their causes. Decide which causes and effects belong together. Draw lines. (You can look back at page 171.)

CAUSES	EFFECTS
Factories, homes, and cars burn oil, wood, and coal.	People are cutting down rainforests to open land for cattle.
People are using poisonous products to clean things or to kill grass.	The ozone is getting thinner.
"Acid rain" falls into lakes and rivers.	There is a lot of CO_2 in the atmosphere.
People are eating more beef.	Fish are dying.
People are using a lot of styrofoam products and air conditioners with CFCs.	There are toxic chemicals in our land and water.

Threads

Remember, this planet is also disposable.

Paul Palmer

LEARNING STRATEGY

Using New Words: If you *use* a word soon after you see it for the first time, you'll remember it better.

B. What are some environmental problems in your country or city? List them here. (Look at page 171 for help with vocabulary.)

Environmental problems in _____:
                                                  (my country)

_____   _____

_____   _____

_____   _____

173

PART TWO:
THE PLASTICS OF THE
FUTURE

IT WORKS!
Learning Strategy:
Getting Information

C. Share your list with a small group. Add other items to your list if you like.

D. Talk with classmates, your teacher, people at your school, and people in your community. Ask them, "What do you do to help the environment?" Complete the chart with their answers.

Asking for Clarification

IF YOU DON'T UNDERSTAND SOMETHING, YOU CAN ASK THE SPEAKER:
Pardon?
What does that mean?
How do you spell that?

PERSON'S NAME	WHAT DOES THIS PERSON DO?	WHY? (HOW DOES THIS HELP THE ENVIRONMENT?)

E. In a small group, discuss your charts. What are people doing to help the environment?

PART TWO: THE PLASTIC OF THE FUTURE?

Before You Listen

A. You are going to hear a report about plastic.* Before you listen, think about your home and everything in it. How many things are made of plastic or have plastic parts? (Bags? Telephone? Packaging? TV/ etc.) List them here.

_____ _____ _____

_____ _____ _____

_____ _____ _____

LEARNING STRATEGY

Understanding Word Parts: If you understand parts of words, you can guess their meanings more easily.

EXAMPLE: *-able* is an adjective ending. It means that something *can* happen.

renewable = something can be new again, over and over

biodegradable = something can become part of the earth

B. Complete the sentences. Choose from these words.

breathable	drinkable
changeable	livable
disposable	recyclable

1. We need to clean up the water so that it will be _____.

2. The air pollution is so bad that sometimes the air isn't _____.

3. There are a lot of toxic chemicals in that area, so everyone had to move out of the neighborhood. The area isn't _____.

4. The weather is very _____ these days. One minute it's warm, and then suddenly it's cold.

5. Don't throw away that bottle. It's _____.

6. New parents like to use _____ diapers for their babies. Unfortunately, Americans throw away 18 billion of these diapers every year, and they aren't biodegradable.

Listening

IT WORKS!
Learning Strategy:
Listening for the
Main Idea

A. As you saw in Part One, plastic is not biodegradable. If you throw away a plastic bag today, it will be here on earth for your great-great-great-great-great-grandchildren. You are going to hear two people talk about a possible solution to the problem of plastic. You won't understand every word. Just listen for the main ideas and complete these sentences.

Right now people produce plastic from _____.

In the future, maybe we can produce plastic from _____.

B. When you're listening for reasons, listen for words such as *first, second, third,* etc. Listen to the report again. Why do people want to harvest (get) plastic from potatoes? Give two reasons.

1. _____

2. _____

After You Listen

A. You are going to read an article about plastic plants. Below are some questions about the article. Look for the answers as you read. There will probably be many words that you don't know, but don't worry. Think about what you *do* understand. When you find the answers, mark them in the article with a marking pen.
   1. In what part of a plant does plastic develop?
   2. In the future, in what part of a plant will there be plastic?
   3. What is a British company making from a biodegradable plastic?
   4. What is the problem with the plastic from the British company?
   5. When will we be able to buy actual products of this biodegradable plastic?

IT WORKS!
Learning Strategy:
Thinking Ahead about
a Subject

Researchers sow seeds, harvest plastic

Guilt-free throwaway plastic bottles, bags and diaper liners could be the fruit of research at two U.S. universities. Scientists have bio-genetically engineered a plant—the green kind, not the factory kind—that makes plastic.

And the plastic is biodegradable: It decays without harming the environment.

"Just like wood," says Charles Downs at Michigan State University, one research site; the other is James Madison University in Virginia. The breakthrough is reported today in *Science* magazine.

Future plastic plants could be a new cash crop for farmers. Now, the plastic develops in the plant's stems and leaves, but researchers hope to produce plants whose "fruit" would be lumps of plastic rather than tomatoes or potatoes.

Plastic already is being made, in factories, from plant products such as cornstarch—but it also contains petroleum.

A British firm makes bottles from a biodegradable plastic grown by bacteria cultures. But the plastic costs about $12 a pound vs. 50 cents for plastic made from petroleum. Plastic grown from plants is expected to cost about $1.20 a pound.

Actual products are still more than five years away.

James Kim, From USA Today (April 24, 1992) page 1A.

Using a Dictionary

> **MANY WORDS HAVE MORE THAN ONE MEANING. THIS SENTENCE FROM THE ARTICLE INCLUDES TWO MEANINGS OF THE WORD** *PLANT*:
>
> "Scientists have bio-genetically engineered a *plant*—the green kind, not the factory kind—that makes plastic."
>
> This dictionary entry has two definitions of *plant*:
>
> **plant** *n.* 1. a life form that is usually held to the ground by roots and makes food from soil, water, and air. Ex. *Trees are large plants.* 2. the machines, buildings, etc. of a factory, business, or institution. Ex. *Automobiles are made in that plant.*
>
> You need to look at a sentence and then choose the correct definition for a word:
>
> She bought a *plant* for the garden.   A lot of people work at that *plant*.
> (*Plant* = Definition 1)   (*Plant* = Definition 2)

B. Choose the correct definition for each underlined word below. Write the number of the definition in the space.

> **earth** *n.* 1. the planet on which humans live. **Ex.** *The earth travels around the sun.* 2. ground; soil; dirt. **Ex.** *He planted the tree in the earth.*

1. Soon we might dig potatoes out of the <u>earth</u> and find plastic in them. (Definition _____)

2. The ozone protects the <u>earth</u> from harmful sunlight. (Definition _____)

> **sow** *v.* 1. plant seed on or in the earth. **Ex.** *The farmer will sow his wheat next week.* 2. plant in the mind. **Ex.** *The enemy agents tried to sow discontent among the people.*

3. They <u>sowed</u> confusion everywhere. (Definition _____)

4. Scientists are <u>sowing</u> seeds to try to grow plastic. (Definition _____

> **culture** *n.* 1. the idea, arts, and way of life of a people or nation at a certain time. **Ex.** *We have learned from the culture of ancient Greece.* 2. a specially prepared material in which bacteria and cells will grow, used in scientific experiments.

5. How do people do this in your <u>culture</u>? (Definition _____)

6. A British company is making plastic in bacteria <u>cultures</u>. (Definition _____)

C. For one week, keep a list of every plastic item that you bring home, throw away, or recycle. Be sure to include plastic containers (such as milk bottles), packages, and bags.

Threads

For referrals on environmental information in 100 countries, contact INFOTERRA, UN Environmental Program, United Nations, New York, NY 10017.

THINGS THAT I BROUGHT HOME	THINGS THAT I THREW AWAY	THINGS THAT I RECYCLED	PART THREE: CREATIVE SOLUTIONS
_____	_____	_____	
_____	_____	_____	
_____	_____	_____	
_____	_____	_____	
_____	_____	_____	
_____	_____	_____	

PART THREE: CREATIVE SOLUTIONS

Before You Listen

You are going to hear a report from National Public Radio* about a city in Brazil. Before you listen, guess the meanings of the underlined words in the sentences below.

1. I don't want to live in that <u>ramshackle</u> area. It's such a horrible, poor neighborhood.
2. He found a job with the <u>municipality</u>. It's the first time that he's ever worked for the city.
3. We recycle all of our <u>non-organic trash</u>—glass, plastic, and metal garbage.
4. The streets used to be <u>filthy</u>, but they're clean now.
5. They <u>transformed</u> the city. It's completely different now.
6. Do you see this machine? They made it from <u>scrap metal</u>. Can you believe that they found all that metal in the garbage and landfills?
7. Each week we <u>separate</u> our plastic and glass from the other garbage. We put the plastic in one large can and the glass in another large can.

Listening

A. Curitiba is a city in Brazil. (You pronounce it "Cureecheeba.") It's a poor city. There are environmental problems. There are also human problems; many people are very poor, and many children don't go to school. But this city is finding solutions to these problems. The mayor, Jaime Lerner, says, "When you don't have the money, . . . you have to be creative." Listen to Section 1 of the report and answer the questions on page 178. You don't have to understand every word. Just listen for the information that you need.

SECTION 1

1. In the neighborhood of Vista Alegre, what do women get from the municipality?
2. What do the women exchange for this?
3. How has the neighborhood changed?

SECTION 2

B. Listen to Section 2 of the report and answer these questions. You don't have to understand every word. Just listen for the information that you need.

    1. In a program called "Garbage that Isn't Garbage," what do people put out for the garbage truck to take?
    2. Men and boys work at the recycling center. Before they began this work, what problem did the men have?
    3. Before they began this work, where were the boys living? What must they now do every day?

SECTION 3

C. Listen to Section 3 of the report. Mayor Lerner says: "Sometimes there is a kind of syndrome of the tragedy in our cities." Then he explains this sentence. What does he say?

_____

_____

After You Listen

Now You Choose. Work in groups of four to five students. Each group needs to choose *one* of the two projects below.

PROJECT 1

1. Imagine that your group is the Environmental Protection Department of Xenrovia (a small, poor country). This country has many environmental problems and doesn't have much money. Make a list of the country's environmental problems. (Air pollution? Toxic chemicals in the water? No more space for landfills? Filthy streets? People cutting down rainforests?) For more ideas, look at your list on page 172.
2. As a group, think of solutions to these problems. Remember, your government doesn't have much money. However, you can write any laws that are necessary. (Use modals in your laws: *may not, must not, must, has to/have to, will.*) Put a copy of these laws in your portfolios.

Threads

Predicted World's Largest Cities in the year 2000 (population in millions):
Tokyo–Yokohama, Japan—29.97;
Mexico City, Mexico—27.87;
São Paulo, Brazil—25.35.

PROJECT 2

1. Imagine that your group is an advertising company. Many environmental organizations have come to you for help. They want you to organize ad campaigns, but you have time to work for only one of these organizations. Choose *one* of these environmental problems:

   a. The African elephant is disappearing.
   b. Air pollution is so bad that the air in this city isn't breathable.
   c. The rainforests are disappearing.
   d. Plastic is piling up in landfills and is not biodegradable.
   e. People are throwing away too much garbage.
   f. People are throwing garbage in the ocean and ocean animals are dying.

2. Organize an ad campaign for this problem.

   a. Think of a good slogan, or saying. (For example: "If you're not recycling, you're throwing it all away.")
   b. Design a one-page magazine ad.
   c. Plan a five-minute program to teach schoolchildren about the problem.
   d. Write a short radio ad to persuade people to change their actions. Record this on a cassette tape.
   e. Put your ads and cassette tapes in your portfolio.

SELF-EVALUATION

You have now finished this book. What have you improved about your listening and speaking? What do you still need to improve?

I HAVE LEARNED ABOUT OR IMPROVED . . .

_____

_____

_____

I STILL NEED TO PRACTICE . . .

_____

_____

_____